Resting in the Waves

also by Doug Kraft

Centering Home

Buddha's Map

Beginning the Journey

Kindness and Wisdom Practice

Meditator's Field Guide

Befriending the Mind

V₅

Resting
in the Waves:

Welcoming the Mind's Fluidity

Doug Kraft

Easing Awake Books

Published by Easing Awake Books, 2020
Carmichael, CA 95608
https://www.easingawake.com

ISBN: 978-1-7350737-0-5 paperback
ISBN: 978-1-7350737-1-2 e-book

I am grateful for
• The cover image created by Jens Troeger using
www.unsplash.com photos by Roberto Delgado Webb and
Erika Varju
• Permission to use "The Little Duck" by
Donald C. Babcock, The New Yorker, © Conde Nast.
• The patient and careful editing of Daia Gerson

Unless noted otherwise, *sutta* translations are from Bhikkhu
Bodhi through Wisdom Publications (199 Elm Street,
Somerville, MA 02144).

Printed in the United States
5 4 3 2 1

Contents

The Little Duck

Now we are ready to look at something pretty special.
It is a duck riding the ocean a hundred feet beyond the surf.
No, it isn't a gull.
A gull always has a raucous touch about him.
This is some sort of duck, and he cuddles in the swells.
He isn't cold, and he is thinking things over.
There is a big heaving in the Atlantic,
And he is part of it.
He looks a bit like a mandarin, or the Lord Buddha meditating
            under the Bo tree,
But he has hardly enough above the eyes to be a philosopher.
He has poise, however, which is what philosophers must have.
He can rest while the Atlantic heaves, because he rests in the
            Atlantic.
Probably he doesn't know how large the ocean is.
And neither do you.
But he realizes it.
And what does he do, I ask you? He sits down in it.
He reposes in the immediate as if it were infinity — which it is.
That is religion, and the duck has it.
He has made himself part of the boundless,
by easing himself into it just where it touches him.
I like the little duck.
He doesn't know much.
But he has religion.

Donald C. Babcock
The New Yorker, October 1947

Introduction:

Welcoming Fluidity

Sometimes I wake up in the wee hours of the night, roll over, and fall back to sleep. Other times I don't drift off so quickly. I'm wide awake. So I get up and meditate. Lila, our cat, curls up in my lap and purrs herself back to sleep. The crickets "purr" in the background.

I love meditating in the quiet of the night. The world feels gentle and smooth. I'm less tempted to push or strain. Thoughts, images, memories, plans, song fragments, feelings, and more ramble through. I don't get caught up in them — at least not for long. And I don't tell the mind to shut up, watch the breath, or even send peace into the world. I'm content letting the mind do its thing without getting entangled in its stories. I relax on the sideline and let the mental parade mosey on down the street. I'm simply aware — nothing more, nothing less.

The Buddhist term for "mindfulness" is *sati*. Sati is sometimes translated as "bare attention," meaning awareness without commentary. Buddhism doesn't distinguish between mind and heart. So sati can also be translated as "heartfulness." Sati means knowing and seeing what's going on and taking it to heart at the same time.

We could call this "welcoming the mind's fluidity." Rather than controlling the mind, we watch it with a clear and openhearted friendliness. Rather than getting engrossed in its content, we watch it flow by.

Do you ever wake in the middle of the night and hang out with the mind? Or lie in a hammock on a lazy summer afternoon and watch the mind drift here and there? Or, on a long drive, gaze outwardly at the scenery flowing by as you gaze inwardly at the flow of thoughts?

If so, you know what I mean by "welcoming fluidity." You watch the mind's drifting with curiosity and an open heart, without getting caught up in the contents.

It sounds simple and innocent. Yet welcoming the mind goes to the heart of the spiritual journey, awakening, and freedom from suffering. It has nuances and complexities that may not be apparent at first glance. Nevertheless, when we truly welcome the mind, it naturally settles into spaciousness, clarity, and contentment.

Welcoming the mind's fluidity is the essence of the meditative process as I understand it. It is also the subtitle of this book. Let's look at what the words connote.

Welcoming

Welcoming a person (or anything) requires two things: seeing them as they are and accepting them as they are.

Clear Seeing

First, we must perceive them truly as they are. If Frank joins our *sangha* (our community) and I greet him with, "Welcome, Bob, it's so good to see you. I've enjoyed your music over the years. It's great to have you with us," Frank might think, *I can't carry a tune in a bucket. And he doesn't even know my name.* I may feel wonderfully welcoming, but Frank feels alienated — as if I've confused him with someone else.

Welcoming someone requires seeing the person with all their beauty and warts, gifts and confusion. Otherwise, we may welcome an idealized image or a caricature, but not that complete person.

Acceptance

Second, to welcome someone, we must accept them as they are. Out of caring, we may wish them more happiness, clarity, or wisdom. But our affection is not diminished by their imperfections. We don't welcome them on the condition that they change. We're open to them as they are.

Acceptance does not necessarily imply approval or disapproval. Moral judgment is a different faculty, which comes later, if at all. If we feel we must judge someone, it helps to see and accept them first before applying a set of values.

Like mindfulness (sati), welcoming requires both seeing clearly and taking what we see to heart, whether we're looking at another person or at ourselves.

Mind

In the same way we might openheartedly welcome a person, the subtitle of this book recommends welcoming the mind. What is the mind? This is not a philosophical or metaphysical query. I'm asking, "In our direct experience, what is the mind?"

The mind is a field of awareness in which phenomena arise, move, morph, and fade. It's fluid rather than stable. This flow goes on constantly when we're awake and often in our sleep.

However, the mind often directs our attention to the content of experience rather than to the process of experiencing. It's as if we're walking through a meadow. We notice a chipmunk on a boulder, a robin swaying on a branch, a stream gurgling near our feet without being cognizant of the expanse of the meadow itself or of the sky as it stretches to infinity. In a similar manner, the mind points attention to what's in the field of awareness more than to the field itself. We often miss the field or, at best, take it for granted. We miss the forest for the trees, the ocean for the waves, the particulars for the context. Sometimes we try to control the mind by directing it to a specific topic. But we rarely just observe the mind to see the pointing itself.

Nonetheless, if you have ever gazed at the mind in the middle of the night or while resting in a summer hammock, you may have sensed the field of awareness itself. If you are a practitioner of certain styles of open-awareness meditation, you already do this intentionally as part of your practice.

Fluidity

Welcoming has practical implications that touch on both meditation and daily living. To put it bluntly, there is no mind. What we refer to as "mind" is a subjective flow of phenomena with no perceived beginning or end.

Realizing this "no-mind" can be unnerving. We want a rock to hold on to or a boulder to stand upon. We may feel like the cartoon character Wile E. Coyote, who chases a roadrunner off a cliff. Wile E. keeps running through the air until he realizes he is suspended far above terra firma and crashes to the rocks below. Then he miraculously recovers and begins the chase anew. But just as Wile never catches the bird, we will never grasp an objective experience of the mind.

To engage in an effective spiritual practice and lead an awakened life, we need two things: (a) a way to connect with the underlying reality of fluidity (i.e., no undergirding self-essence and no solid mind); and (b) when we get a glimpse of this fluidity, we need to embrace it without freaking out and clinging to the delusion of solidity. In other words, how do we relax into the freedom of no-self and no-mind? How do we rejoice in the fluidity of never-ending change?

Even though there is no solid, enduring self or mind, it still helps to welcome the qualities that do arise — to be open to and accepting of fear, anger, ease, delight, infatuation, etc. There is nothing personal about them. They are hardwired biological responses. They are automated signals. We can't control what comes into the mind, and we can't control the biological responses that result.

Even though we can't control them, we don't have to indulge them either. We don't have to get caught up and carried away. The easiest way to do this is to see and accept the responses as they are. Then we can stand back rather than act them out. We can't get rid of the signals. Welcoming means seeing and accepting them as they are without getting lost or entranced.

This helps us gradually stop identifying with the contents of the mind and see it as a flow and a process. In the long run, the attitude with which we greet the mind can have a profound effect on contentment and well-being. It doesn't change the contents in the moment. But ultimately, seeing the larger field enriches our lives.

Resting in the Waves

A more poetic way to express this is "resting in the waves." Meditating in the middle of the night with my cat curled up in my lap as I gently watch the ebb and flow of the mind-heart without getting entangled in it ... that is the essence of resting in the waves. Trying to stop the whitecaps in our lives is as impractical as trying to calm the heaving of the sea of life itself. The ocean is vast, extending far beyond the horizon. We sit like ducks in the expanse.

The heart of spiritual practice is as humble as sitting down. As the poet and philosopher Donald C. Babcock put it, we "repose in the immediate as if it were infinity — which it is." Rather than try to rise above the ocean, the duck "made himself part of the boundless, by easing himself into it just where it touches him." That is freedom.

I hope this book helps you rest in oneness.

> *Text blocks like this are sprinkled throughout the coming pages. They suggest exercises that bring the subject more deeply into direct experience. As you read, you may want to stop and engage these contemplations. Or you may wish to read them lightly and come back to them later. Or not at all. Please use them in ways that support you best.*

1

Fluidity of Self

My computer had a meltdown: My email accounts flickered, the contents of my calendar disappeared, my backup drives sputtered. I spent hours on the phone with Apple support trying to sort it out. I was not a happy camper.

If you had asked me who I was in the middle of that, my answer would be very different from the one I'd give if you had asked me in the middle of the night while I was meditating with my cat. And those two selves are different from the me hanging out with my grandson on the beach. And those selves are different from the one bicycling along the American River, or choosing cereal in the grocery store, or delivering a dhamma talk.

I do not have *a* self. I have *many* selves. And so do you. So do all of us.

> Ask lightly, "Who am I?" "What do I experience directly in this moment that I label 'me'?" "Who and what am I really?"

Weather

We usually think of mind and self as solid entities. But the mind is a process, not a thing. *Self* is a verb, not a noun. The mind and self are less like entities and more like the weather: ever-changing, uncontrollable, and impersonal.

When we lived in New England, the weather could shift dramatically from day to day. "If you don't like the weather," we'd say, "just wait a few hours."

Now we live in Northern California, where the changes are usually gradual. Still, the weather is fluid, even if the rate of flux is slower. And we have little influence on what the weather will be. We can hope, wish, complain, pout, demand, or pray to the weather gods. But the weather is indifferent to our preferences. It obeys natural laws, over which we have no dominion.

Nevertheless, climate change is real. While we have no control over today's weather, how we relate to nature has significant influence in the long run. When we oppose natural laws, the cumulative effects are not pretty.

Similarly, we have little control over the mind in the short run. It, too, obeys natural laws over which we have no dominion. But how we relate to it has a powerful influence as time goes by. If we try to control the mind, or try to fix it, oppose it, or condemn it, the results likewise are not pretty. But if we relate to it with wisdom, kindness, and respect, it becomes more peaceful, content, and wise.

Since most of us identify with the mind and its perceptions, our sense of self is also fluid, beyond our direct control, and impersonal.

The suffering mind gets stuck on things. The awakened mind-heart rests comfortably in the ever-shifting flux of experience, like the little duck riding the ocean.

Welcoming fluidity is about cultivating an open and caring attitude toward our ever-changing sense of self and ever-fluid mind. It can deepen, open, and enrich our lives.

Multiple Selves

The thought of having multiple selves can be disconcerting. But having many selves is normal. The difference between most of us and someone with clinical multiple personalities is amnesia. Someone with multiple personality disorder can't remember what happened when they were identified with a different persona. Most of us can remember. We may not have the same personality at work that we have when playing with our kids or hiking in the mountains, but we remember those experiences.

Self-identity can be strongly influenced by circumstances. There was a period in my life when I had two starkly different jobs. I had left the ministry to become a psychotherapist. It would take a few years to develop a full-time counseling practice. Meanwhile I had bills to manage. So I took a part-time job as a software engineer in a large computer company.

On Mondays, Wednesdays, and Thursdays, I drove to an industrial park, walked into a catacomb of office cubbies, and spent the day interacting with high-speed computers and high-tech folks.

On Tuesdays and Fridays I went into my home office and spent the day listening to clients and their struggles as we sorted out their selves and the meaning in their lives.

I enjoyed both jobs. When I recognized how differently I experienced myself in each job, I mused, "Am I crazy?" Yet when I was engaged in either job, I felt perfectly normal.

The various circumstances in your life may not be so starkly disparate. But they probably are not homogenous either.

> *Close your eyes and imagine the various situations you move through each day. Note the attitudes, perspectives, thoughts, feelings, joys, stresses, and views of life that feel natural in each situation. Whom do you experience yourself to be when you are with a close friend, at work, playing with children, listening to the evening news, walking in nature, sitting in class, or in other settings?*

Persona therapy is a school of psychology (developed by Carl Jung, Eric Berne, and others) that works intentionally with all our various selves. It helps name the numerous personalities and identify their needs. Then, as we flow in and out of them, we can take better care of them all. This can deepen well-being, contentment, and joy. Persona therapy suggests that becoming aware of and having a good relationship with all of our selves helps us to have a good relationship with life.

Authentic Self?

This begs a question: Is one of these personas our authentic higher self? Or is there another, truer self-essence — our "soul," if you will — hidden behind all these fluid selves?

> *When you ask, "Who am I?" note your answer and follow up with "Who or what experiences this self?" Note that answer and follow up again, "Who experiences that self?"*

Most of the world's religious traditions say we have a soul essence. Vedānta, Hinduism, Judaism, Taoism, Christianity, Islam, and others say the purpose of the spiritual journey is to discover our real, higher self or soul. They suggest this essence survives bodily death to enter another life or another realm.

Through meditation the Buddha came to a radically different conclusion. He said that none of our personas is carved in stone. They grow, change, and evolve. Ultimately there is no fixed self-essence, just fluctuating self-identities. Self is an ephemeral, fluid process, not a tangible entity. It might better be labeled "selfing" (an action) rather than "a self" (a thing).

If the Buddha was right, the near universal belief in a soul-essence may be an evolutionary distortion. Ancient ancestors who believed they had a self-essence to protect were more likely to survive and reproduce than those who were convinced they eventually dissolve like mist in the morning sunlight. The belief in an eternal self or soul motivates us to survive and reproduce.

> *What if there is no experiencer apart from experiencing? What if selfing is real and self is a distortion? What if selfing is primary and self is a secondary by-product? Sense the implications.*

In the end, the Buddha was not interested in philosophical debate. He felt it was more important to explore the phenomena and see what they revealed. He encouraged us to drop all concepts and notice directly the experience we call "mind" or "self," "minding" or "selfing."

So let's do that. Let's take a step closer to what's going on inside and explore our experience. In this chapter, we'll consider two related topics:

1. What is self-sense? That is, what sensory impressions give rise to a sense of self? While many factors shape our various selves, there are a few key elements without which our selves would seem radically different. What are they?

2. What is the function of self-identity? Rather than go down the rabbit hole of speculating "Who am I?" or "What am I?" we'll explore our various selves as coping mechanisms for dealing with life's variety.

The following chapter brings the Buddha's practice into this exploration and looks at his insights into these issues. Subsequent chapters reflect on the practical implications of welcoming the fluidity of the mind, awareness, and spiritual practice.

Sense of Self

But first, what gives rise to a sense of self? Many experiences affect our self-sense. But there are two elements without which self-identity would not arise at all: neural binding and a specific type of neural suppression.

Neural binding has to do with several sensory experiences merging into one mental event. This helps simplify the vast complexity of the world into manageable "objects." A bird lands on a branch outside my window and chirps. My subjective experience is of a single bird that flies, lands, and sings. I don't perceive this as separate objects: one that flies, one that sits, and one that chirps. Neural binding is how the brain combines several phenomena into one subjective object or cohesive story.

Neural binding also plays a key role in our sense of self. Here's an example:

I'm sitting in a chair giving a talk. Sometimes I use hand gestures. Other times my hands rest on my lap, one hand on the other. I'm not conscious of my hands because I'm busy attending to what I'm saying. Yet my hands are not numb. If I purposely put my attention there, I feel them well enough. But mostly I don't notice my hands.

Now you come up quietly behind me, reach out, and softly touch my hand. I notice your touch instantly. I might even stop midsentence and turn to you to see what you want.

This scenario seems ordinary. But when we think about it, it's curious. The touch of your hand on mine is similar to the sensation of me touching my own hand. Yet your touch grabs my attention while my own touch flies below the radar. How come? The explanation is complex:

The motor cortex sends signals to muscles in the arm telling them how to move in such a way that one hand lands on the other. As this signal travels down a nerve, it bifurcates before leaving the skull. One branch goes back into the brain. The second branch leaves the skull and goes to the appropriate muscles. Then, as the muscles move, they create sensory signals that are sent back to the brain.

Meanwhile, the first branch that goes back to the brain searches memory for sensations that have been produced by those muscle movements in the past. These expectations are sent to the sensory centers of the brain.

So when I move my arm, the sensory centers receive two sets of signals: one from the brain telling it what to expect and the other from the muscles telling it what is actually happening.

When the sensation of movement neurally binds with the expectation of movement, it's as if the brain understands, "I touched my hand." If there is no expectation to bind with the actual movement, the brain understands, "I didn't touch my hand. Something else must have touched it."

The brain responds differently to these two situations. If the actual sensations are close enough to the expectations, reflexes that could be triggered are ignored or suppressed. I barely notice that one hand has touched the other. This is neural suppression.

Tickling

The poster child for neural binding and neural suppression is tickling. If I'm ticklish and you rub my sides or underarm in a particular way, I giggle and squirm. I don't want to be tickled. I don't want to giggle and squirm. But I can't help it. It's a biological reflex.

However, if I rub my side or underarm in the same way, I get no tickle reflex whatsoever. I feel the rubbing. But now those sensations are neurally bound with the expectation of those sensations. The tickle reflex is completely suppressed. I can't tickle myself even if I want to.

Worm

The neural binding and suppression occur on a very basic level. They are precognitive. We see them in very simple organisms.

If I poke an earthworm with a stick, it pulls away. I doubt it cogitates before moving — its brain is hardly any larger than a single ganglion. It doesn't have enough neurons to ruminate. Its withdrawal is reflexive.

However, if an earthworm bumps into a stick, the pressure on its skin from the collision is nearly identical to the poke from my stick. Yet it doesn't pull away.

If the worm withdrew every time it touched something, it would never get anywhere! Its survival depends on avoiding some sensations and ignoring those same sensations when they are generated internally. Without eyes or ears, it relies on touch to navigate. How does it distinguish between it touching something and something touching it?

The answer is neural binding. Like us, the worm generates an internal signal of what its body movement should feel like. If there is no neural signal to expect those sensations, the withdrawal reflex is triggered. If the expected sensations are neurally bound with the actual touch, the withdrawal reflex is suppressed. This combining of the two signals is so important that it is highly automated. This is neural binding and neural suppression.[1]

And it is the beginning of a sense of self and other. The worm can make some simple distinctions between itself and the environment. I doubt it ponders, plans, or fantasizes about itself — it hardly has enough brains for that. But it can make the rudimentary distinction between "me" and "not me." The worm withdraws in response to something touching it, but it doesn't withdraw in response to it touching something.

---

[1] Neuroscience calls this the "efferent copy," the copying of the outflowing (efferent) signal that then branches back to the brain. If the expectations from the efferent copy are close enough to the actual (referent) sensation, any reflexes that could be triggered by the actual sensations are ignored or suppressed. However, the effect is very short-lived. If an expected sensation arrives even a second late, the suppression doesn't happen. The signal is treated as if it came from "out there" rather than "in here."

These expectations are probably learned rather than preset by the genes. At least in humans, very young infants show no sense of self. They have to learn what to expect from their bodies.

Furthermore, the tiniest lesions in the brain can disrupt this mechanism. Some symptoms of schizophrenia may be the result of the brain not properly processing the efferent copy. Schizophrenics may "hear" their own thoughts as if they arose from the environment. They report "voices in their heads," which are probably actually misattributions of internal thinking.

> *Where does your sense of self seem to reside?*
> *Does it center in your head behind the eyes? From where*
> *you look out at the world, "down" to the body, and "up"*
> *to the top of the head?*
> *Or does it center in the chest? From where you look*
> *sideways to the arms and "up" to the head?*
> *Or is it dispersed throughout the body?*
> *If it seems to center more in one place than another, let*
> *your awareness go into that place. What do you notice?*
> *If there is any tension in that place, let it relax.*
> *Surrender. What happens?*

Coping Mechanism

Neural binding and neural suppression occur in relatively simple creatures. They also happen in us. But our neural network is so much larger that our sense of the self and the world are vastly more complex.

For example, as I write these words, I'm cognizant that ice shelves off the coast of Greenland are melting; there are riots in the streets around the world; my cat just jumped onto my lap and is kneading my leg; my fingers are typing out words; a faint hunger echoes in my stomach; I hear a jet plane in the distance; a space heater near my feet just turned on; my toes feel chilled; I remember angry political debates in the news; one of my family members is sick; my car is out of gas; the sun glows through the leaves of the trees in my yard; a towhee just landed on the bird feeder outside my window; and so much more. At any given moment there are thousands of events far and near.

The Buddha spoke about four "imponderables" (*acinteyya* in Pāli). One is the complexity of the universe. It is more intricate, multidimensional, and diverse than we have the brain cells to process. If we try to sort them out all at once, our nervous system overloads and shuts down. The Buddha called this "vexing."

Fortunately, evolution bred into us a mechanism that buffers us from overload. The brain tries to filter stimuli and allows into awareness only that which is most relevant to the moment. It does this so quickly and quietly that we usually don't notice the shifting process. We just refer to it as "who I am." Our sense of selves becomes a coping mechanism for managing the variety of situations in our lives.

If I am with my sangha discussing Buddhist practices, certain attitudes and perspectives coalesce into a self-image that helps me attend to what is most relevant while I'm in the group.

If a fire alarm goes off, suddenly my self-image shifts from "dhamma student" to "flammable being." I don't carefully ponder and decide to shift mood, alertness, focus of attention, and so forth. It just happens. My self-sense flows effortlessly from one set of qualities to another.

When I'm talking to a computer-support specialist, reading a bedtime story to my grandson, or hurrying through traffic, my self-identity flows to different sets of qualities. It's a coping mechanism that helps me adapt to the fluidity of the world around me.

On the other hand, if I am strolling through a meadow on a quiet day or soaking in a hot tub in the evening, life is easy and my sense of self softens and fades. There is little challenging me for the moment, so a sense of self is not needed. It recedes into the background or disappears.

Our sense of self is fluid both in how it adapts to different situations and in how it becomes denser under threat and fades when life is mellow.

> Notice the strength of the self-sense as it waxes and
> wanes through the day. When you notice any tension in
> it, gently relax the tightness and observe what happens.

Dysfunctional Selves

If we were always wise, aware, and our coping mechanism worked smoothly, we'd be enlightened. We'd adjust optimally to each situation and life would be groovy.

But we are works in progress. Human evolution isn't perfect. Things go wrong, slip out of balance, or break down. This can result in a loss of fluidity — we get stuck for many reasons. Sometimes the sense of self helps us navigate a difficult situation. Sometimes not so much.

One reason we get stuck is that evolution is slow and changes in human society are rapid — particularly in the last few thousand years. Natural selection wired biological reflexes into us that may no longer be relevant. For most of our evolution, we were puny creatures in a world of giant predators. The biological reactions that helped us survive in old environments are often not relevant now that we are the alpha predator at the top of the food chain. Some wired-in responses are outdated.

Another reason we can lose fluidity is trauma. Difficult events can lock our system into patterns that continue after the stressor has passed.

Let's look at a broad spectrum of dysfunctional selves and what may be helpful and healing for each.

Stuck and Runaway Minds

On one end of the spectrum are people who have difficulty taking care of themselves because of schizophrenia, psychosis, severe thought disorder, or biochemical imbalances. The mind freezes up or runs away in obsessive thinking.

Optimal treatment for them might include medication and/or psychological techniques designed to bring errant behavior and thought under control. For these people, insight meditation is probably not optimal. It may help some, but doesn't address the core problem.

"Ordinary" Neurosis

If we move from that extreme up to the middle of the spectrum, we come to ordinary neurosis: people who can manage themselves in the world pretty well but have exaggerated fears, anxieties, or other emotional imbalances. For these people, the optimal strategy is not pharmaceuticals or behavioral control. It is loosening up and opening up. It is going more deeply and kindly into bottled-up feelings and getting them exposed, expressed, and released.

Sometimes milder medications, such as the serotonin reuptake inhibitors (e.g. Prozac, Zoloft, Paxil), may help take the edge off so the person can open more. But the basic strategy is not chemical. It is gaining more understanding of how one's own system works and disinhibiting emotional blockages wisely. Direct insight can be very helpful. Meditative awareness can be healing.

Well-adjusted Malcontents

As we move toward the upper end of the spectrum, we find people whom the early-twentieth-century mystic, philosopher, and teacher George Gurdjieff called "well-adjusted malcontents." They have adapted to the world, can care for themselves just fine, but yearn for more spiritual depth. They are seekers.

Many strategies look for a deeper, higher, truer self. Erik Erikson's psychotherapy extends into these higher reaches as does Maslow's hierarchy of needs. Hinduism, Ayurveda, some Christian mystical schools, Native American spirituality, and more speak about finding a higher self. For years I channeled a "higher being," who directed me toward my true self until I began to see that "true self" was not the highest possibility.

There are many helpful forms of meditation that support this search for a higher self. They tap into and support the yearning for a deeper, richer experience of life.

Non-Self

At the top of the spectrum is nondual awareness or non-self — when no essential distinction is made between self and other. Buddhism is basically nondual in its understanding of life and in its deepest meditation practices. As such, it's not the most appropriate strategy for all people and all imbalances.

The Harvard psychologist Jack Engler once said, "You have to love yourself before you can lose yourself." If we have a poor self-image or painful feelings, trying to get rid of our painful self is just aversion. We have to deal with the discomfort rather than push it under the rug. To go beyond a sense of self, we must genuinely love ourselves and then recognize that there is deeper truth beyond the self.

> *Look at the world through the eyes of a child.*
> *Then look through the eyes of a wise elder.*
> *Now look through the eyes of nobody.*

Don't-Know Mind

To summarize, self-sense can either be a coping mechanism that keeps our life on track or a distortion that derails us. It can also be both and neither.

Self is like a shimmer in the air on a hot afternoon. Water vapor subtly bends light that passes through it. The vapor is invisible — we can't see it. All we can see is the distortion it causes.

"Who am I?" is a compelling question that evades easy answers. We can't see vapor, only its effect. We can't see the distorter, only the distortion. We can't see self, only the effects it has on experience.

Self-sense is invisible because it arises out of preverbal, preconceptual, precognitive suppression of sensation. It arises out of something we aren't aware of rather than out of something we sense.

A Sufi story tells of a man looking for his key in the grass outside his house. A friend comes by and helps him search. When they can't find it, the friend asks, "Where did you lose it?"

The man answers, "Inside."

"Why are you looking out here?"

"The light is brighter."

An earthworm doesn't have the bright light of a complex neocortex that can think, ponder, imagine, and expound. Yet it has a functioning self. We, like earthworms, have a functioning self. It doesn't arise out of something we sense. It arises out of a rudimentary, preconscious suppression of sensing. We'll never find it in the bright light of thought.

When I was a beginning Zen student on retreat, the Korean Zen master Seung Sahn gave me the kōan "Who am I?" When I meditated on it deeply, it took me into a place of not knowing who I really was. That don't-know mind is closer to the truth than any neocortical concepts or fantasies. Kōan training invited me to welcome and relax into the imponderable not-known. This is where wisdom begins.

Seung Sahn asked, "Who are you?" I answered, "I don't know!" He smiled and gave me the next kōan.

> *The next time you encounter something you don't know, rather than resist the blankness, relax into it.*

Freedom from Self

The Buddha had many insights into self and the process of welcoming fluidity. But he spoke to a prescientific, agrarian culture, while we live in a postindustrial society. He had a different worldview and spoke a language with an entirely different structure. Nevertheless, he had deep insights that can help us today.

So in the next chapter we'll bring his teachings into the discussion. We'll consider some of the ways he viewed and spoke about this topic. In the end, his message is direct and simple: There is no freedom for ourselves; there is only freedom from a self.

> *Although immeasurable, innumerable, and unlimited beings have been liberated, truly no being has been liberated. Why? Because no bodhisattva who is a true bodhisattva entertains such concepts as a self, a person, a being, or a living soul. Thus there are no sentient beings to be liberated and no self to attain perfect wisdom.*
>
> — Buddha, *Diamond Sutra*
> translator, Mu Soeng

2

In the Buddha's Words

How would you summarize the Buddha's teaching in a word or simple phrase?

I've posed this question to several Buddhist sanghas. It's a bit outrageous given the thousands of pages of text attributed to the Buddha. But the sangha members were good sports and offered words such as the following:

Mindfulness

Paying attention

Awakening

Staying present

Enlightenment

Kindness

Impermanence

These familiar Buddhist terms are good suggestions. My first contribution to the list was not so familiar: "process" or "everything is in process." As I contemplated further, I settled on an even less familiar phrase: "welcoming fluidity."

In this chapter I'd like to unpack what drew me to this phrase and why I think it's a fair translation of the Buddha's core message. And we'll look at some of the other terms he used that may not be familiar in everyday English.

But before doing that, let's consider the problems inherent in any translation of his teachings into English.

Prakrit, Pāli, and English

In the Buddha's time (circa 500 BCE), there were many different languages and dialects in and around the Ganges River Valley. People didn't get around easily as we do today, and, with the relative isolation, varying dialects evolved.

The Buddha probably spoke Magadhi Prakrit — that is, the dialect of Prakrit spoken in the ancient city of Magadhi. But he wandered far during his half century of teaching, and therefore it's likely that his followers spoke a number of different dialects.

Years after this death, his monks chose the Pāli language to be the uniform repository of his talks as they began to write them down for the first time. Pāli and Prakrit are similar, but not the same.

At that time, sacred teachings were not written down. They were transmitted orally because spoken language was more nuanced and offered more refined expression. Writing was considered coarse and appropriate only for mundane topics that required little nuance — inventory lists and business contracts.

His talks were passed by word of mouth from generation to generation. Like the modern children's game of Telephone, verbal transmission is vulnerable to having the meaning drift. It was six hundred years before these oral talks were finally committed to writing in Sri Lanka.

Therefore, it is important to remember that as we read the Buddha's words, we are reading English translations of

Pāli translations of the Magadhi Prakrit spoken several millennia ago.

Language was used differently back then. The Buddha lived long before the scientific revolution. Language in his day was more evocative than it was definitive. It was used to evoke meaning rather than to pin it down in a scientific formula.

Also, Pāli has a lexicon of about fifty thousand words while English has well over a million. For every word in Pāli there are an average of twenty words in English. Pāli words thus have to cover a broader range of meanings. Trying to pin each down to a precise definition is not helpful. Even English words have multiple meanings.

It also helps to know that English has a higher percentage of nouns than most languages, while Pāli has a higher percentage of verbs. Many Pāli terms translated into English nouns are actually gerunds, words that in English end with "—ing." Furthermore, Pāli has no articles — no "the," "a," or "an" — which make nouns sound even more solid. The phrase "welcoming the mind" in Pāli might be worded more literally "welcoming minding." Pāli is more fluid than English.

Because of these translation issues, the best way to discern finer points of the Buddha's teaching is to hold the meanings of the words loosely and see how they compare with our own experience. This may not feel satisfying if we want the assurance of precise definitions, but it's the best we can do.

Process

With this in mind, let's turn to the idea that "process" and "everything is in process" might serve as good candidates for summing up the central theme of the Buddha's teachings.

The word *process* does not appear very often in Buddhist texts, and for a good reason: The Pāli language has no word for it. It's not in the lexicon.

The Buddha seemed to be saying that *everything* is in process. But without a word for it, he had to use metaphors such as "impermanence," "arising and passing," "dependent origination," "changing," and so on.

If we look inside at our own subjective experience, we won't see solid objects — just an ongoing flux and flow of experience. We cannot trace this flow back to any origin. And we cannot see any final destination. We may imagine both a start and an endpoint, but we don't experience either — just a flux and flow. Some changes are rapid — they arise and pass in a few moments. Some evolve slowly over years. Yet the mind keeps morphing in subtle or dramatic ways.

It can be unsettling to think we do not have a solid self or a unitary mind essence to hold on to. So we imagine them. Yet in the moment-to-moment flow of actual experience, there is no objective mind or self, just subjective, shifting experiences. This shifting obeys the law of cause and effect. But the essence of the mind and self are ever-changing: They're processes, not things.

> What if self is not a thing but a process? Not a subject nor an object but a verb? What if when the process stops, there is no thing (nothing)? What if self is a by-product of experience rather than the experience being a by-product of self?

Anicca, Anattā, Dukkha

Since there was no word for "process" in the Pāli or Prakrit lexicons, the Buddha's central teaching of "the three characteristics of all things" is referred to with metaphors. In Pāli, the three are *anicca* (impermanence), *anattā* (no unchanging self), and *dukkha* (suffering). These three can be reduced to one English word: "process." Here's how:

All three Pāli words are negations. This was a common rhetorical device in the Buddha's time; rather than state what something is, we state what it isn't. This forces us to engage more deeply to discern what the positive quality might be, particularly if we don't have a word for the positive.

Anicca means "impermanent." The prefix "a-" is a negation in Pāli. Literally the term means "not permanent," or "everything is in the process of changing from one thing to another." A positive way of saying this is "fluidity." The first characteristic of all things is that they are ever-changing, or fluid.

The root of the word *anattā* is *attā*, which means "self" or "higher self." The prefix "an-" is a negation. So *anattā* translates literally as "non-self" or "not self." Not only is everything impermanent but the self that perceives is also impermanent. Self is a fluid process. Another valid translation of *anattā* is "not personal" or "impersonal."

Put anicca and anattā together and we get the first two characteristics of all things as "everything is fluid including the self that perceives" and "everything is impersonal." It's not about *me*.

The third characteristic, dukkha, means "suffering." Dukkha literally refers to a wheel in which the hole for the axle is off center. As the wheel turns, it presses and grinds. In other words, from time to time, life presses and grinds.

The etymology of the word reveals another meaning. The root *kha* means "patience." The prefix *du-* means "without." So *dukkha* literally means "without patience." When we are impatient, we suffer. That's definitely true!

Dukkha underscores the importance of anicca and anattā. If we don't see the fluid, impersonal nature of all things, including the self that perceives anything, life will press on us — we're going to hurt. On the other hand, if we have patience — that is, if we are more welcoming of whatever comes along — then we suffer less.

Sati and Mettā

The Buddha's primary concern was relieving suffering. When he said, "Everything is in process" (anicca and anattā), he was not making a metaphysical claim. He was suggesting a way of looking at life as ever-changing. He advocated cultivating direct insight into how things really are. Meditation is a process of helping us see simply and accurately how life is.

As mentioned in the introduction, two Pāli words commonly associated with his meditation are *sati* and *mettā*.

Sati means "mindfulness" or "bare attention without commentary." However, since Buddhism makes little distinction between mind and heart, *sati* can also be translated as "heartfulness."

Mettā (Sanskrit: *maitrī*) is often translated as "loving-kindness." However, the word ordinally meant "friend." So *mettā* is more accurately translated as "friendliness." Mettā is not a highfalutin or formal loving-kindness but a simple, ordinary friendliness. As a verb, the idea of friendliness implies "welcoming."

"Welcoming fluidity" means cultivating clear, openhearted friendliness. Rather than trying to control life or getting engrossed in its contents, we watch its flow.

Ownership and Control

This attitude is implicit in the Buddha's view of ownership. His view was common in the East during his time and is still common in many native cultures around the world. It says that we own only what we create and control. The West has a much more expansive idea of ownership that includes things we didn't create and don't fully control.

For example, when Europeans began settling in the Americas in the 1600s, they offered trinkets for large parcels of land. They thought they were buying real estate owned by local tribes. They thought that ownership meant jurisdiction over the land, how it was used, and who could live upon it.

To those native Americans, the land was owned by the gods or the Great Spirit who created it and the natural forces that work upon it. The countryside itself was available to be used by all who hunt, gather, or live there. Humans could no more control land than they could control the seasons or how life grows and dies. The gift of trinkets just meant they would all share the land together. It didn't mean the Europeans could overpower Mother Nature or had the right to drive others off. The land was owned and controlled by the gods, not the tenants.

In his own time, the Buddha also linked ownership to control. This point is central to the following colorful vignette in the *Majjhima Nikāya 35*.

In the sutta, Saccaka is a renowned and brash debater who picks a public fight with the Buddha. Referring to various aspects of the body and mind, Saccaka says, "I assert thus, Master Gautama: 'Material form [i.e., his body] is my self, feeling tone is my self, perception is my self, thoughts are my self, consciousness is my self.' And so does this great multitude [of people listening to us]."

Saccaka uses the debater's trick of appealing to the prejudice of the audience. The Buddha responds, "What has this great multitude to do with you? Please confine yourself to your own assertion."

The Buddha continues, "I'll ask you a question in return. Answer it as you choose… Would a head-anointed noble king — for example, King Pasenadi of Kosala or King Ajātasattu Vedehiputta of Magadha — exercise the power in his own realm to execute those who should be executed, to fine those who should be fined, and to banish those who should be banished?"

Saccaka agrees that kings have such power.

The Buddha continues, "When you say, 'Material form is my self,' do you exercise any such power over that material form as to say, 'Let my form be thus; let my form not be thus?'" For example, can Saccaka turn his arm into a wing?

Saccaka remains silent.

The Buddha presses him for an answer, saying, "If anyone, when asked a reasonable question up to three times by the Tathāgata [the Buddha], still does not answer, his head splits into seven pieces there and then." A spirit holding an iron thunderbolt appears in the air above Saccaka. Saccaka is terrified. "No, Master Gautama," he concedes. "I can't make my form [i.e., his body] be anything I want."

The Buddha seems to rub it in. "Pay attention to how you reply! What you said afterward does not agree with what you said before."

The Buddha goes on, "When you say, 'Feeling tone is my self,' do you exercise any such power over that feeling as to say, 'Let my feeling be thus; let my feeling not be thus?'"

"No, Master Gautama."

The Buddha continues through perception, thoughts, and consciousness.

The Buddha wins the debate. But he continues with a Dhamma teaching: Since all aspects of the body and mind are impermanent and subject to change (that is, they're fluid), adhering to them leads to suffering. He says, "When one adheres to suffering, resorts to suffering, holds to suffering, and regards what is suffering thus: 'This is mine, this I am, this is my self,' could one ever fully understand suffering or abide without suffering?"

Saccaka concedes. In the words of the sutta, he "sits silent, dismayed, with shoulders drooping and head down, glum, and without response."

The sutta ends on a positive note. After conceding several more Dhamma points, Saccaka acknowledges that he has been "bold and impudent." He embraces the Buddha's teaching and offers a meal to the Buddha and his followers as a way of expressing gratitude.

Not Metaphysical

Notice that the Buddha is not making a philosophical or metaphysical claim. He is just defining ownership as having control. Since we ultimately don't have control over the body or mind, we don't own them. If we don't own them, they certainly are not us. They are not mine, me, or myself.

His logic is compelling even if the conclusion is disconcerting. Most people tacitly assume they own the body and mind they live with.

Just because we can't control them doesn't mean they are out of control. They obey natural laws. If we understand these laws and work with them, we can influence the body and mind. We can give it food to abate hunger. We can give it rest to lessen fatigue. We can give it medicine to reduce illness. We can meditate to soothe thoughts. We can influence the body and mind. But they are not ours. And we are not them.

Familiarity

The idea of ownership can be overstated. The word *mine* doesn't always imply control. When I say "my wife," or "my kids," or "my tree," I'm not claiming I control them. An ordinary citizen of Kosala may refer to Kosala as "my town" without any illusion of being in charge.

Sometimes the word *mine* just means "it's familiar to me" or "I welcome it." Perhaps we confuse familiarity with ownership and self-identity. I am familiar with my family. The Kosalans were familiar with their town. All of us are familiar with "our" bodies and minds. We travel with them all the time.

I like the phrase "The mind has a mind of its own." It's helpful to think of the body and mind as travel companions. If we relate to them in a welcoming manner and get to know the natural laws that govern how they work, we can exert some influence.

But in doing this, we are obeying natural laws rather than trying to control or make the laws. This helps us navigate life rather than try to control it. We are the navigator, not the pilot. We have influence, but not full control.

The Senses

Ownership, control, and familiarity are related to the senses. Through sense perception we know the world around us and the relationships between "out there" and "in here."

Western science describes five senses. The Buddha described six. I find it helpful to consider seven.

Organ	Object	Sensation
Eyes	Colors & Shapes	Seeing
Ears	Sounds	Hearing
Nose	Scents	Smelling
Tongue	Flavors	Tasting
Skin & Body	Felt Objects	Touching
Mind	Thoughts	Thinking
Body	Emotions	Feelings

The first four senses have discrete organs associated with them: eyes, ears, nose, and tongue. The fifth has a generalized organ: the skin. It also includes the body in general. Some touch sensations are not felt by the skin but arise deep inside: nausea, headaches, muscle soreness, etc.

For the Buddha, the sixth sense modality is thinking. The "organ" is the mind, which does not have a discrete place in the body. In the West, many believe thoughts arise in the head — we have a lot of tension there that draws attention. But other cultures view thoughts as arising in the chest or nowhere specific. The Western attribution of thoughts to the head is probably the product of culture rather than of physiology.

The Buddha was not naïve — he acknowledged that mind sense is different from the physical senses. But for the purposes of training, we can treat it the same way we treat the physical senses: The organ is the mind, the object is thought, and the sensation is thinking.

> *Try observing the thinking process apart from its content. Does it seem to arise in some part of the body? If so, relax that area and see what happens.*

As mentioned earlier, the Buddha made little distinction between thoughts and emotions or between mind and heart. They are conjoined for purposes of spiritual training.

However, as a psychotherapist, I find it helpful to treat emotions as a seventh sense. Emotions can arise throughout the body. Anger tends to start in the pelvis, rise up the back the way an animal gets its hackles up, and move out into the arms and fists and up into the teeth, which get bared, and the eyes, which glare. Fear, on the other hand, tends to drop down the front of the body. Excitement can spread throughout the body, including into the fingers and toes. Compassion arises in the chest and flows up into the arms and head. And so on.

What is most important in spiritual training is not adopting a Western view, a Buddhist view, or my view. The Buddha was not interested in philosophical debate. What's important is seeing how we relate to these sensory modalities and how they operate in our own experience.

Which experiences do we identify with, thinking, *This is me. This is myself?* And which ones do we relate to as being "out there" and "not me"? And finally, which experiences are in the middle ground — not something that I own but something I feel I own and should control?

For most people, the discrete senses are "out there": I see a sunset, hear a bird, smell a fragrance, and taste some ice cream. Touch sensations, on the other hand, feel more personal. We are more comfortable touching someone we feel close to than we do a stranger.

Thoughts and emotions may float back and forth between me and not me. Some people identify closely with their thoughts: "This is just who I am." Others may not: "I don't know where that thought came from." Similarly, some people identify closely with their feelings while others may sometimes see them as foreign intruders.

Nevertheless, the more clearly we observe the various sensing modalities and our responses to them, the more we see them dispassionately as phenomena that arise, morph, and fade. They are merely experiences that come and go. They are not "me, mine, or who I am."

This is probably why the Buddha treated thought and emotion as a sixth sense that we can experience the same way we know physical sensations. This gentle dispassion helps us awaken.

> *How do you relate to your body? Do you see it as you? ("This is me, this is myself.") Or do you see it as something you own? ("These are my hands and my feet.") Or is it merely a familiar travel companion? How do you relate to thoughts? Are they you or something you own or just a companion? How do you relate to emotions?*

Welcoming Fluidity

If we welcome life and its laws, we can be with them and experience natural contentment and ease. But we don't own life. We are part of it rather than it being part of us. We obey life, or we pay the consequences. Life doesn't obey us. We are under its control. Life is not under our control.

Therefore, a welcoming attitude toward experience and its natural fluidity is essential to living peacefully with life as it is. It goes to the heart of the spiritual journey, awakening, and freedom from suffering.

3

Fluidity of Mind

Sometimes we don't know what we know. Someone asks me, "Was Jill there the other night?" I say, "I don't think so." But I pause, relax, and let images of the meeting drift into memory. "Oh yes, she was in the third row on the right."

The knowledge that she was present was stored somewhere inside. But it took a while for me to access it.

There is a lot that we know without knowing it. A growing body of research documents how information, attitudes, feelings, and inclinations affect us even when we can't bring them into conscious awareness. But with the right tools — hypnosis, meditation, drugs, mental exercises, patience, etc. — we can sometimes access data stored in the shadows of the mind.

There is no hard line between what we know consciously and what we know unconsciously. Information, attitudes, and more come in and out of the shadows all the time. And there is no hard line between what we know consciously or unconsciously and what we don't know at all. We can potentially learn new things anytime.

The Mind Is Not the Self

Awareness, the mind, and our various selves mix and flow together and interact with one another in ways suggested by the diagram on the following diagram.

I use the term *awareness* to refer to all that we know consciously and unconsciously, explicitly and implicitly, knowingly and unknowingly. It is a vast landscape that extends beyond the horizons of the mind.

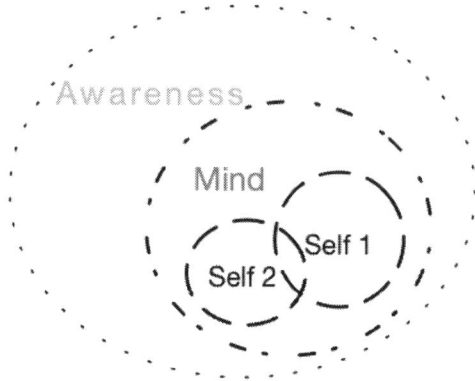

Awareness

Mind

Self 1

Self 2

I use the term *mind* to refer to what we know or remember consciously. At first, Jill was in my hidden awareness, but not in my mind. After reflecting, she came to mind as being at the meeting. The boundaries of the mind are quite fluid. What we know we know can expand and contract.

I use the term *self* to refer to the small subset of the mind with which we currently identify and through which we perceive.

One of the reasons various selves can be so fluid is that each draws a small sampling from the mind and the mind draws from the vast field of awareness. The self that sings a silly song to a child draws on a different set of memories, attitudes, feelings, and inclinations than the self that balances the checkbook. The self that argues politics draws on a different set of factors than the self that comforts a friend.

Some of the selves may mingle and overlap, but they aren't the same.

In this chapter we step back from the small, fluid self and look at the larger phenomena of the mind and its fluidity.

The Mind Is Not the Brain

The brain has what the philosopher Alfred North Whitehead calls "simple location" — we can find it in objective three-dimensional space and time. We can point to where our brain sits inside our skull.

But the mind doesn't have simple location. Thoughts, worries, inspirations, and images are real, but we can't point to where they are.

For example, have you ever seen a blue chicken?

Neither have I. But now there is an image of a blue chicken in my mind and I'll bet there's one in yours. It's real, but it doesn't have simple location. I can't see your chicken and you can't see mine. They exist in the subjective realms of the mind and its imagination, not in the shared objective external world of the brain.

There is a connection between the brain and the mind. Synaptic activity in various parts of the brain correlates with various subjective experiences. But the connection is mysterious — we have no idea how it works. We don't even know which is the cause and which is the effect. Does the thought of a chicken cause a certain pattern of neural firing? Or does the neural firing create the thought? We don't have a clue.

Happiness, contentment, wisdom, and well-being arise within. They don't have simple location. So if we want these qualities, we must work with them internally in the mind.

Four Ingredients

As we discussed earlier, when we openly and clearly see the processes of the mind-heart, we see four ingredients or factors that shape its content and workings:

1. The world around us

2. Wired-in proclivities

3. Personal history

4. Willpower

Let's look at each of these.

1. The World Around Us

The first factor is the world around us. It has a huge influence on the mind. To put it bluntly, *we have very little control over what enters or leaves the mind*. We may like to think we're in charge, but we aren't. We have a little influence, but not much effective power.

For example, don't think about that blue chicken — put it out of your mind…

Try a little harder…

The harder you try to get rid of it, the more vivid it becomes.

Where did the bird come from? …

It came from me. More precisely, when you read my words "blue chicken," it showed up uninvited in your mind. Now, it's like the man who came to dinner — you can't march it to the door and throw it out.

There are two strategies for getting rid of the chicken. One is to concentrate on something else — perhaps a green gopher. If you zero in hard enough, one-pointed focus will push the chicken away. But it takes a lot of effort and may leave you tired and irritable.

I practiced one-pointed concentration on the breath for twenty-five years. Sometimes the strain left me irritable: If someone broke my concentration, I didn't like it.

Another strategy to get rid of the chicken is to just let it be, without making a big deal of it. Relax with it in a friendly way. In a while, the chicken may fade. But whatever the case, the amiable attitude allows the mind to ease up, open, and feel better, whether the chicken stays or goes.

The lesson of the blue chicken is that we don't have much control over the mind. But with a welcoming attitude, we have some influence.

We can thank Mother Nature for minds we cannot control. Consider two prehuman ancestors strolling through the primordial forest several million years ago. They spotted a saber-toothed tiger in the distance. The sight was upsetting.

One of them had the ability to put the disturbing thought out of his mind. He focused on the sunny sky and the food they were looking for. The other was paranoid. In his distress, he couldn't stop thinking about the tiger.

Which one's DNA do you think we inherited?

The first lived a short, happy life and was eaten before she/he reproduced. The second had a long life mixed with pleasure, pain, and many children. We are her/his descendants.

Evolution bred into us minds that reflect the world around us whether we like it or not. If our minds misrepresent the world, we are like bats flying without sonar.

We aren't always thankful for minds we can't control. The cultural stereotype proclaims the value of independence — we want to be the captain of our ship. But as captain, we actually only have a little influence. We can set the sails and turn the rudder. But the nature of the ship, the ocean, the winds, and the weather have a greater effect.

And quietly we have derogatory words for people who ignore their surroundings: "out of touch," "narcissistic," "not grounded in reality," "crazy," "self-centered," "lost in their own world," and so on.

If we are lost in our inner, subjective experience, we are less likely to survive and reproduce. So we've been bred to be affected by what goes on around us. The world "out there" has a strong impact on the flux and flow "in here." Sometimes the impact is wholesome. Sometimes not so much.

> *When a sensation (e.g., the sound of a bird or a car) enters your meditation, how often do you get absorbed in the perception? How often do you push it away? How often do you just observe?*

Though the forces of evolution gave us responsive minds, they also gave us many biases. This brings us to the second ingredient of the mind.

2. Wired-in Proclivities

To support our survival and reproduction, our minds need not perceive with total accuracy. It can be an advantage to exaggerate some impressions and ignore others. Some distortions may be upsetting. But if they don't interfere with survival or reproduction, evolution doesn't care because our genes get passed along anyway.

In other words, as the mind maps reality, the map may be distorted. We have no control over these biologically based biases. They happen, and vary from one person to another. But if we understand distortions as distortions, we needn't be fooled by them.

The most obvious distortions and omissions are the result of the limitations in our sensory equipment.

For example, bats emit high-frequency squeaks, which bounce off objects around them. Their sensitive ears use these echoes to map the vicinity. They can track and catch a flying mosquito.

I can distinguish the difference between the acoustics of my garage, a room of stuffed furniture, and an ocean bluff. But track and catch a mosquito in the dark? I'm comparatively deaf.

My cat has great long-distance vision. But like most cats, she's farsighted – close objects appear blurry. However, her sense of smell is vastly more acute than mine. When she enters a new yard or room, she carefully sniffs to create a map based on odors. She takes one whiff of a person or animal and remembers it accurately years later.

I can distinguish the aromas of fresh-baked bread, a sweaty friend, and a mown field. But using fragrance to discern whether the animal hiding in the bush is a cat, squirrel, chipmunk, or dog? Forget it.

I find it hard even to imagine a map of the world based on sounds or smells. The operative word here is *imagine*. We humans are visual creatures. Most of us have five physical senses but rely heavily on sight. We think more in terms of images than sounds, smells, tastes, or touch. From miles away I can easily see the difference between a seagull, a hawk, an airplane, and a blimp.

We like to think our visual maps are complete. But in truth, they include only a tiny spectrum of reality. We translate this selective sensory information into thoughts that represent the world. These maps are sparse representations.

Other distortions are not based on sensory information but on the perception of threats, enticements, or confusion. These give rise to liking, disliking, and ignorance. Let's look at these proclivities.

Threats

As we create thought-maps, we distill and distort them further. If something is perceived as a threat, the mind highlights it. The threat might be physical, social, or emotional. Rather than using a red highlighting pen, the mind uses attention-grabbing emotions: fear, anger, disliking, or other aversive qualities. This is not something we can control. If something could potentially be a threat, uncomfortable emotions will arise automatically. They just happen.

For example, I was in the kitchen musing about something when my hand brushed against a hot grill on the stove. Instantly the musings evaporated as awareness honed in on my throbbing finger.

The shift from daydream to injury was instantaneous. I didn't reflect, *Hmmm. Maybe I'll come back to these musings later. For now, I think I'll see what's going on with that burning sensation.* Rather, attention shifted immediately and reflexively.

Burns, cuts, bumps, bruises, or anything that threatens the integrity of the body grabs our attention by highlighting it with negative emotions.

The evolutionary advantages of these wired-in reactions are obvious. There are rare neurological disorders in which people don't feel pain. Their instinct to avoid injury is stunted. They don't do very well in the world.

When asked, "Why do we suffer?" the Burmese meditation master Sayadaw U Tejaniya quipped, "We need the motivation."

The threat can be physical or social. We are creatures who rely on others. The "Visual Cliff" experiment illustrates how deeply social instincts are bred into us.

Researchers built a table with a big hole in the middle.

They covered the table and hole with plexiglass. Then they placed a baby on the plexiglass and let him crawl around. When he came to the hole, he faced a paradox. Visually the hole looked like a cliff he was about to tumble off. But tactilely, it felt solid. The scientists wanted to know how he would deal with the ambiguity.

All the infants solved the problem the same way: They looked for their mothers. If the mother looked upset, the baby backed away from the apparent danger. If the mother was calm, the baby crawled over the visual hole.

This social instinct has an obvious evolutionary advantage. Intelligent creatures require a more complex brain, and a complex brain requires a long time to mature. Simpler creatures, such as bees, are born as adults. But intelligent animals require years for their neurology to fully develop.

As a result, during infancy and childhood, we are relatively helpless. The strong social instinct to look to others for cues is one way we manage. Even more important, parents have strong, wired-in instincts to look out for their children. Without these social instincts, the parents' DNA in their kids would die out before it reproduced.

Anything that disrupts our social bonds can signal threat and trigger aversive emotions that grab our attention. Even the look of disapproval in the eyes of a friend can set off our inner alarm.

Enticements

If there are no discernible physical or social threats, aversive emotions may remain quiescent. Our inner alarm is quiet.

However, if something around us can support our health or reproduction, our neural system highlights it with attraction, liking, or other pleasant feelings. Good food, soothing music, a stimulating story, a potential sexual partner, and more can suffuse the body with pleasure and urge us to move toward the source of pleasant feelings.

Neuroscientists find that we are four times more sensitive to threat and pain than to enticements and pleasure. When our distant ancestors had to choose between running from a giant wolf or reaching for a piece of fruit, those who ran away survived better than those who grabbed the food and ignored the predator.

So fear and aversion have a stronger impact than attraction and liking.

Threats and enticements — dangers and attractions — are the most obvious distortions. There are many subtler biases that have served evolutionary purposes too. Anytime there is distortion in our perception, there is some tensing or tightening behind it.

Confusion

If there are no obvious sources of threat or nurturance, but something is ambiguous, the mind highlights it with curiosity, confusion, or tentativeness. These encourage us to look more closely.

Liking, Disliking, and Ignorance

In Buddhism, these three kinds of distortions are called hatred, greed, and delusion — or liking, disliking, and ignorance. They are deeply automated. That is why it's so hard to not think about a blue chicken: Trying to get rid of the chicken is an aversive action, which tells the mind there is a threat. The threat draws attention to the chicken even if this is not our conscious intent. And if we find this frustrating, that is more threat.

But if we relax and let the thought be there, the inner alarm quiets down. In time, the mind loses interest and the thought fades.

Notice that turning the alarm off is not the same as ignoring the signal. Seeing a man running toward me with a big stick sets off a threat alarm. If I try to ignore the alarm, it doesn't work. If I look more closely and see that he is smiling and the stick is just a baton from a relay race, I realize my fear is a distortion. I can relax and the alarm quiets.

It is wise to pay attention to alarm signals — not just to the situation but to the signal itself and what is causing it. If it points to a real threat (e.g., I left the stove on), then we can deal with it. But if it's a false alarm, we will see the distortion as distortion. That allows the mind to relax.

In the text, the Buddha describes the source of suffering in the Second Noble Truth with the Pāli word *taṇhā* — a subtle or obvious tightening of the body, emotions, or mind. If we can relax that tension, the distortion dies down.

> *By simply observing the flow of experience, notice when the mind highlights some things and dismisses others. As you notice the emphasis, does the tension in it soften by itself? If not, see what happens when you intentionally relax.*

Cognitive Bias

So far we've looked at distortions based on sensory limitation and on distortions from the big three wired-in signals — aversion, attraction, and confusion.

But there are many smaller cognitive biases. For example, we tend to trust the opinion of someone we like more than someone we dislike. We tend to believe mass media has a stronger effect on others than it does on us. We tend to believe we can discern other people's motivations better than they can discern ours. We tend to give more credence to information that supports our views than to information that undermines our opinions. There are hundreds of cognitive biases that have been researched and documented.[2]

---

[2] The online encyclopedia *Wikipedia*, lists hundreds of carefully researched cognitive biases. Daniel Kahneman's book *Thinking, Fast and Slow* (2011) gives detailed explorations of many of these.

We cannot remove many biases and distortions. They are wired in. However, if we are aware of the bias, we can adjust appropriately. We can recognize that our perception is slanted and not be taken in by it. We can't avoid bias, but we don't have to be fooled by it. And with practice, the biases may weaken too.

> *Which proclivities (impersonal reactions in your mind) are difficult to notice as they arise? Which are easy? Which seem personal? Which are impersonal?*

3. Personal History

There are other distortions that are not as deeply wired in but are nonetheless powerful. These arise out of our personal history.

I grew up in a family where there was little abuse but some emotional abandonment. It shaped my system. Today, my responses to an abusive remark tend to be well measured and with little distortion. But my responses to emotional abandonment can be exaggerated. Despite years of therapy, meditation, and reflection, it's still easy for me to feel left behind or ignored.

However, today I find it easier to recognize these reactions without getting carried away. It's easier to see the biases as biases and not be taken in by them. I still feel them, but take them less personally. They have subsided, but the flavor lingers.

There are entire libraries on personal psychology and the myriad ways life experience can alter our perceptions and motivations. For the purposes of this writing, I'll just mention that being aware of these forces and seeing them realistically is important to spiritual freedom. We may never unwind them completely. But by understanding and

respecting their nature, process, and effects, we are less taken
in by cognitive distortions. Cultivating this clarity is part of
living a mature spiritual life.

> *What in your personal history may distort how you*
> *perceive the present? What are some of the distortions?*
> *How can you deal with them wisely?*

4. Willpower

It is difficult to overestimate the effects on our minds of
the world around us, wired-in proclivities, and personal
history. These forces are mostly beyond our control. But we
are not completely bound by them. This brings us to the
fourth ingredient of the mind: willpower. Willpower can lift
us beyond the constraints of environment, biology, and life
experience.

Western cultures put great emphasis on will. But it is
puny compared to the first three ingredients. Empirical
research suggests that will operates like a muscle. If we use it
heavily over a short period of time, it tires and weakens. If
we use it modestly over a long period of time, it grows
stronger.

For example, most diets require some effort. If I'm
surrounded by family and friends who are on the same diet
or are supportive of my dietary aspirations, it is easier for me
to stay with it. However, if I visit relatives for the holidays
who are drinking, eating rich foods, and consuming sweets,
it takes more effort for me to stick with my program. There is
a greater likelihood that my willpower will be used up and
I'll start eating foods that are less healthy.

Will is a precious resource that is best used humbly,
wisely, strategically, and patiently. Many of the Buddha's
teachings and practices from Dependent Origination to

agenda-less awareness to the benefits of supportive community rely implicitly or explicitly on conservation of effort. The Buddha never suggested we use will as a blunt-force instrument to force ourselves to lean one way or another. Rather, will is used sparingly and intelligently.

There are many practical implications for conservation of effort that we'll explore in later chapters.

> *How much willpower do you use in meditation? When is this unwholesome and generating more distractions? When is it wholesome and contributing to peace and clarity? When is it both?*

Increasing Fluidity

As the mind relaxes and becomes more perceptive, experiences of both the self and the mind become fluid. Part of what makes for a healthy mind and a healthy self is fluidity of awareness — the capacity to adapt easily to changing circumstances.

4

Fluidity of Awareness

Buddhist meditation is about awareness.[3]

What if awareness is a primary property of the universe? A more common assumption is that awareness is secondary. We live in a materialistic culture that sees physical stuff as fundamental and awareness as a by-product of sense organs, neural networks, and brains. When the body shuts down, we assume awareness disappears.

We haven't always thought this way in the West. To the medieval church, for example, the unseen realms were more important than the physical world. Heaven and hell, angels and demons, God and the devil were more significant. They were the puppet masters and we humans were their marionettes on strings.

Modern science turned this on its head, concerning itself only with what we can verify empirically. Arguably, science has done more to relieve suffering than any other human endeavor: Infant mortality rates dropped, life expectancy rose, diseases were cured, food production increased, and

---

[3] Consciousness is about interpretation of what's in awareness: labeling and cataloging our experience. But Buddhist practice is grounded in raw, uninterpreted awareness.

technology made life cushier with everything from airplanes to cellphones to hearing aids to artificial hearts.

Scientific materialism is so pervasive today that we assume that the tangible stuff we can see must be more real than the invisible awareness that does the perceiving.

What if that assumption is wrong? What if awareness does not arise out of our bodies? What if it preexists?

The Buddha did not take a stance on this. That was not his style. He advocated a middle way that sees reality as more nuance, without taking a stance on which is more real.

But as a practical matter, he proceeded as if awareness is primary. He was not interested in philosophical or metaphysical discourse. He was interested in direct experience — in exploring phenomena without intellectual bias. He was a phenomenologist whose spiritual practices tacitly asserted the importance of pure awareness. If we can see our actual experience accurately without distortion, that is enough to liberate us from suffering. He promoted direct, unmitigated, clear awareness as the bedrock of spiritual practice.

Unborn Awareness

Today, a growing collection of data suggests that awareness may not require physical bodies at all. Perhaps our bodies pick up, amplify, and distort awareness, but they don't create it any more than the lungs create the air we breathe or the eyes create the light we see. Awareness might be inherent in the universe itself.

The Buddha referred to this as "unborn awareness." Awareness is not born, manufactured, or created. It has always existed. It can't be born because it's already here. And it can't die.

This is a working hypothesis I'd like to explore. I would not ask anyone to accept this blindly; the world has enough dogmas and theoretical stances already. But if awareness is more fundamental than neurology, this has practical implications for how we engage spiritual practice and life. Knowing these implications is helpful whether or not this working hypothesis is true.

We'll get to the implications in a few chapters. But first we need more context. To provide this, first we'll look at "born awareness." We've already explored our multiple selves and how our biology magnifies and distorts awareness by placing an emotional charge on threats, enticements, or confusion to highlight and draw our attention to them (pp. 46–49). In this chapter we'll look more deeply at the most persistent distortion: the notion of a separate, independent self. The Buddhist story of Bāhiya of the Bark Cloth offers insights into what he meant by self*less*ness — the lack of an autonomous self-essence.

Next, we'll explore awareness without distortions. Over the past fifty years scientists have scrutinized the reports of people who were brain-dead for a short time and then resuscitated. These reports are relevant, provocative, and inspiring.

Finally, we'll look at the spectrum of awareness that runs from highly distorted awareness, to clarity, to the fading of awareness into *nibbāna*.

After exploring these topics, we'll be in a better position to reflect on the implications that fluid, unborn awareness has for spiritual practice and deep living.

True Self?

Perhaps the most pervasive source of tension is the sense of a separate, independent self. Have you ever tried to find your true, authentic self? We assume it must be inside us, but we rarely actually look for it.

One way to do this is to close your eyes, take a deep breath, relax, and look for an experience of "self" within moment-to-moment awareness. Perhaps you notice sounds, but those aren't the self. We naturally deduce that a self must be there somewhere to do the hearing. But all that's actually there is sounds and hearing.

Similarly, we can experience touch sensations, but we can't touch a self that is separate from the sensations. We reason it's there to feel the hardness or softness, warmth or cold. But touch sensations are tangible, while the self is not (see *Majjhima Nikāya* 148).

Contemporary psychologists have studied these sensations in depth. In the middle of the twentieth century, the Swiss psychologist Jean Piaget broke new ground while studying the development of intelligence in children. He recognized that we are not born with a sense of self or even an understanding of separate objects, but that, instead, these are learned.

Piaget carefully observed his three young children. For example, he held a brightly colored ball in front of his infant son. His son looked at the toy and reached out. Then Piaget covered the ball with a blanket. It was within the child's reach, but temporarily hidden. His son turned away as if the ball didn't exist. Out of sight was literally out of mind.

Piaget found that children younger than eight months were "perceptually seduced." It takes a while to develop "object constancy" — the cognitive ability to know something exists when it is not in immediate awareness. Without object constancy there can be no self-constancy — no sense of a self as an object in the world.

Piaget discovered that intelligence (the capacity to process and make sense out of our experience) begins at the point of contact between an organism and the environment. Those sensations are all that we know directly. From them we deduce what is "out there" causing the sensations and what is "in here" perceiving them. "Self" and "other" are logical deductions, not direct experiences.

To see how modern neuropsychology has clarified the physiological mechanisms that underlie these deductions, refer back to footnote 1 on page 17.

> *Close your eyes and look for the flow of actual awareness. See if you can see how there are only phenomena. Can you see self and world as logical deductions, but not tangible experiences?*

Bāhiya of the Bark Cloth

One of my favorite Buddhist teachings about self revolves around a character named Bāhiya of the Bark Cloth (found in Udāna 1.10).

The moniker "Bark Cloth" suggests Bāhiya was a follower of the Bṛihadāraṇyaka Upanishad. *Bṛihadāraṇyaka* literally means "the great forest." Followers of this Vedic scripture revered trees: They communed with them, wore them as clothing, and so on. Wearing bark may make Bāhiya seem like an eccentric kook to us, but he was actually a well-respected teacher with a large following.

The central practice in the Bṛihadāraṇyaka Upanishad was searching for the true, higher self or atman. Bāhiya had pursued this practice unsuccessfully for years.

The Buddha recognized Bāhiya as a sincere yogi searching for an inner self he could not find. So the Buddha said, "Bāhiya, in seeing there is only seeing." In other words, Bāhiya could experience seeing, but couldn't experience a self that is seeing because it does not exist.

The Buddha made a distinction between the relative world and absolute reality. In the relative world of social conventions, of course we have a self and want to behave wisely, take responsibility for our actions, and so forth. But in absolute reality, there is no atman, no higher self, no soul essence, no separate self of any kind. In direct experience there is only the flow of phenomena.

To drive this point home, the Buddha continued, "In hearing, there is only hearing. In touching there is only touching. In smelling there is only smelling. In tasting there is only tasting."

It's difficult to translate the Buddha's words accurately and gracefully into English because, as noted in chapter 2. English has a higher percentage of nouns than most languages, while Pāli has a higher percentage of verbs.

The Buddha is saying that selfing arises out of many, many processes in the web of life (or, more accurately, "webbing of living"), and that these processes interact lawfully through causing and conditioning — or we might say, processing within processing. But there are no independent objects. There is sensory experiencing, but no self doing the experiencing. There is thinking, but no self thinking the thoughts. There is selfing, but no self doing the selfing. There is just interacting flux and flow.

He concludes, "Knowing this fully is the ending of suffering."

Suddenly, Bāhiya got it! He had been unable to find his absolute, higher self because it was not there to be found. And he knew this not as just a philosophical talking point. He knew from years of searching unsuccessfully to find it.

In that moment, Bāhiya woke up. He became fully enlightened.

In the next moment, a bull gored Bāhiya as it ran by and Bāhiya died.

The Buddha said Bāhiya died liberated. He had completed his search by realizing, with direct unborn awareness, how life was.

> *What if self is a by-product of experience rather than experience being a by-product of self? What if self is only a practical tool and not an absolute reality? A moment in time that fades into eternity? When you relax into any experience, does it lose its solidity?*

Near-Death Experience

Bāhiya awoke a few moments before he died — that is, he became enlightened just before his body failed. Some people wake up after they die. Perhaps, as our bodies and neurology shut down and only unborn awareness remains, it is easier to see life without the biases of emotion and conditioning. It is easier to wake up partially or entirely.

This may sound like pure speculation. But there is a growing body of empirical evidence that points in this direction.

One type of evidence is so-called near-death experience. "Near death" is a misnomer because many of these experiences are not *close* to death. They *are* death. Science describes death as the absence of respiration, heartbeat, and brain function: the lungs stop, the heart stops, and the brain shuts down, leaving a flat EEG.

When these three processes quit, the body dies but does not instantly disintegrate. It takes a while for tissue to break down. Under ideal conditions, a person can be dead for as long as a half hour and still be revived without residual damage. Such situations involve a nearby medical facility that can lower the body temperature and artificially keep blood oxygenated and moving until organs are repaired and everything is restarted.

A significant number of people who die and are resuscitated have memories of the time they were dead. Sometimes they report events taking place in their immediate vicinity, like conversations doctors and nurses where having in the operating room when they were dead. Sometimes patients recount events farther away, like what loved ones were doing in the next room or across town.

Science currently cannot account for how a person can remember events that occurred while they were brain-dead. Yet the accuracy of many of these memories has been verified for people of all different ages, religions, education levels, races, socioeconomic positions, and more.

Over the last forty years, hundreds of researchers have scrutinized these reports. Many conventional explanations have been proposed, including oxygen deficiency, seizure, carbon dioxide buildup, endorphins, psychedelics, brain cell disinhibition, hallucinations, dissociation, wishful thinking, personality disorder, dreams, birth memory, medication, deceit, psychosis, hypnotic induction, and religious conviction. All these possibilities have been studied and discredited.[4]

The emerging consensus is that awareness can exist without a living body.

People who die, get resuscitated, and remember being dead usually emerge changed. They have more depth, less fear, greater clarity, more compassion, broader equanimity, brighter energy, opened hearts, natural generosity, and a deep sense of social justice. They have taken a long step down the road to enlightenment.

This suggests that if we want to wake up, one strategy is to die — which is obviously not what I'm advocating. The problem with "death as a spiritual practice" is that the vast majority of people who die stay dead. There is a whole spectrum of approaches to metaphorical rebirth that have a better track record than literal death. To get some perspective on these, let's look at the spectrum of awareness itself.

Spectrum of Awareness

Distorted awareness, a sense of self, unborn awareness, and beyond can be thought of as a spectrum from coarse to subtle types of awareness. They are not separate and distinct but instead relate to one another fluidly, as shown in the table on the next page.

Let's step back and look at this entire spectrum. Knowing where we are in it can be interesting. But knowing how different types of awareness flow from one to another can deepen our lives and heighten our well-being. So we'll look at the various forms of awareness with an emphasis on what

---

[4] For an overview of these theories see David O. Weibers, *Theory of Reality* (2012).

helps each one transition into its neighbor. We'll explore the differences between content, process, qualities, and more. And we'll examine what facilitates the natural flow between them.

Spectrum of Awareness illustrates types of awareness. We move fluidly between these or may be in several at once.	
Type of Awareness	*Examples*
Non-awareness: ⌄ ⌃	nibbāna
Fading of awareness: ⌄ ⌃	neither perception nor non-perception, "winking out," cessation…
awareness of *Awareness:* ⌄ ⌃	spaciousness, stillness, emptiness, Tao, presence without self, unborn awareness, timelessness…
awareness of Wholesome & Unwholesome *Qualities*: ⌄ ⌃	joy, uplift, kindness, generosity, curiosity, peace, compassion… angry, fearful, worry, hurry, dullness, subtle moods…
awareness of *Processes:* ⌄ ⌃	thinking, fighting, planning, arguing, worrying, explaining, imagining…
awareness of *Content*:	thoughts, ideas, concepts, stories…

From Content to Process

The coarse end of the spectrum is dominated by the content of awareness without recognition of awareness itself. One of the complaints of meditators is the difficulty of stopping thoughts and stories from traipsing through the mind. If we believe we are supposed to be in charge of the mind, then these bands of wandering stories and marauding ideas are unwelcome invaders.

On the other hand, if we don't identify with them, seeing them as no more than a passing parade, they aren't a problem. They are just phenomena. We shift attention from "What?" to "How?" — from "What is going on?" to "How do these thoughts arise?" We shift attention from the contents of the mind to the processes active in it. Rather than getting entangled in the plot line, we start to notice that the mind is thinking, worrying, explaining, complaining, bragging, dialoguing, berating, or whatever.

As we notice the activity in the mind, the content may fade into the background. Processes are subtler. As we notice them, awareness gets clearer and less encumbered.

At the same time, tension (taṇhā) in the body, mind, and emotions subsides. So another way to move up the spectrum is to relax tension. The "Six Rs" is a technique that softens tightness wisely by *Recognizing* what's in the mind, *Releasing* it or just letting it be, *Relaxing* any tension, *Re-Smiling* or bringing up uplifted qualities, *Returning* to our home practice, and *Repeating* these six as often as needed. In the next chapter (pp. 89–92) we'll look more closely at meditation practice and explore this technique in detail.

> *When the content of the mind predominates, relax and notice the process generating the content: reflecting, describing, arguing, etc.*

From Process to Quality

As we notice the activities in the mind, we may start to notice the qualities of awareness behind the actions. The easiest qualities to notice may be tension and ease. It's helpful to watch for them. As we see them, they may differentiate into more nuanced qualities.

Tense qualities are traditionally called "unwholesome." They are tight, or tend to generate tension. They come in many varieties: fear, anger, worry, mental thickness, agitation, liking, disliking, dullness, and so on. They feel sticky.

Relaxed qualities are traditionally called "wholesome." They have little tension or move in the direction of relaxation: openness, kindness, compassion, generosity, joy, peacefulness, ease, and so on. They don't feel sticky.

As we continue to relax and open awareness, the unwholesome qualities recede and the wholesome qualities become more apparent. It's tempting to identify with the qualities. They seem so personal that we may fashion a self out of them. But we didn't create unwholesome or wholesome qualities. They just appeared when the conditions were right. So it helps to see them objectively as "anger" rather than "my anger," "fretfulness" rather than "my fretfulness," "longing" rather than "my longing," "peacefulness" rather than "my peace," or "joy" rather than "my joy."

As we notice the qualities, the processes may fade into the background. Seeing qualities and moods impersonally is the beginning of selflessness (anattā) or seeing the impersonal nature of experience.

> *When you are aware of the processes in the mind, relax into them and notice the qualities of awareness: tension, ease, thickness, flightiness, speed, sluggishness, etc.*

From Quality to Awareness of Awareness

As attention moves from content to processes to qualities, the object of awareness — what we are attending to — gets subtler and more refined. If it keeps moving in this direction, all objects begin to fade into the background or disappear. We could call this "pure awareness," because it is awareness without anything in it. Without an object, awareness turns back on itself: awareness of awareness. It's hard to describe because language is too coarse.

It's as if we're walking through a large field. There's such a cacophony of life to observe that, at first, it helps to focus attention by noting: "oak tree," "butterfly," "flower," "grass," "ladybug," "blue jay," etc. As we relax, seeing, hearing, and feeling become more nuanced. The labels that helped steady attention become unnecessary — even distracting. So the naming fades into the distance. There is an easy stream of phenomena without commentary. The observed and the observer (us) merge into an unnameable flow of suchness. This is a taste of pure awareness of awareness.

> When you are aware of the qualities of awareness, relax into them and be aware of awareness itself.

While it's possible to describe awareness of awareness poetically, it's not easy to recognize experientially. We've been bred not to notice it.

From the perspective of evolutionary survival of the fittest, the function of awareness is knowing the external world — recognizing threats to avoid and opportunities that help us thrive and reproduce. In a rough-and-tumble environment, the more alert we are to our surroundings, the more likely we'll pass our DNA along to the next generation. Awareness of awareness itself is mostly irrelevant.

Nevertheless, since pure awareness is a silent partner supporting all awareness, it still lies within us. We retain the capacity to discover it. It undergirds all wholesome mind qualities. The Buddha found that it is quite healing: it is wise, soothing, uplifting, and clarifying. He designed practices that point toward this fluid, infinite presence.

While there are many practices that can help us become more aware of awareness, many meditators aren't familiar with them. So, to give a feel for what they can do, let's go into how two of them work: absence of thought and micro-gaps.

Absence of Thought

When pure awareness first became noticeable in my meditation, I did not find it inspiring or uplifting. I found it confusing and befuddling. I didn't know what was going on.

At that time I had been meditating several times a day for twenty-five years. Yet I still quietly believed that "good" meditation should be free of thought. Nevertheless, no matter how I practiced, the mind kept chatting, gurgling, whispering, sputtering, yelling, and otherwise spinning out stories, concepts, and ideas. I couldn't make it stop.

Finally, I capitulated — I resigned myself to never being an adequate yogi. I adopted what years later I learned was an old Tibetan practice. But at the time, I wasn't guided by Buddhist teachings, Tibetan or otherwise. I was guided by a growing desperation and sense of futility. Thoughts were the enemy, and I was losing the battle. Since I couldn't win, I decided I might as well learn more about my adversary. Rather than trying to stop the thoughts, I observed them to see what I could learn. Rather than pushing them aside, ignoring them, or trying to relax them into oblivion, I'd just be with them. I wanted to know what thoughts were — not their content but their substance. What was the essence of thoughts? How did they start? Where did they come from? How did they arise?

I retreated to quietly observe, like a naturalist hiding in a tree with binoculars and a notepad. And when I did …

… nothing happened …

For the first time in my life, there were no thoughts. They disappeared. I sat looking at a blank inner landscape. I waited for thoughts to poke up their heads. They didn't.

Gradually, my mind dulled. Immediately, the countryside was populated with stories and commentaries running all over the place. But I never saw them arrive.

I brought clearer awareness to the menagerie. They disappeared. It was like playing whack-a-mole, but rather than whacking furry critters, I was trying to see thoughts and where they came from. But when I looked closely, they vanished.

I spent two years at it. Every time I relaxed and opened up, the thoughts hid under rocks. When my attention dulled or tightened a little, mental images, songs, and paragraphs popped up. The irony of this was not lost on me; when I wanted to be rid of thoughts, they appeared; when I welcomed them, they disappeared.

Finally I got it: The thoughts were triggered by subtle tension. Without tightness, mental processing stopped. The core of all thinking — the ingredient without which it could not exist — was gross or subtle holding, tightness, or thickening of awareness. The Buddhist term for this was *taṇhā*. The Buddha's second meditation instruction (the so-called Second Noble Truth) was "Taṇhā is to be abandoned." When I abandoned tension (i.e., relaxed), thinking disappeared and there was nothing left but awareness itself. Without something to grab hold of, awareness turned back on itself: awareness of awareness.

I had not gotten the full benefit of this because I had been quietly convinced that I was doing something wrong.

Yet, even somewhat pure awareness is soothing. It soaked into my practice over those two years. I lost interest in evaluating my progress as I enjoyed the emerging peacefulness.

As the mind settles and moves up the spectrum of awareness from content to processes to qualities, we needn't be surprised if moments of pure awareness emerge spontaneously. This knowingness is always present within coarser experience. It has no ax to grind, no agenda to promote, no inclination to jump up and down or draw attention to itself. As we relax, the activity in the mind dissipates, leaving behind only awareness. We can't find pure awareness by trying to find it. Yet it can emerge at any moment. It may be much simpler than we suspect. It doesn't seem holy or esoteric. It seems ordinary. It feels beginningless and endless. It is Lao Tzu's untranslatable Tao. ("The Tao that can be spoken is not the true Tao.") It is unborn awareness. It is presence without a self. It is everything and nothing, transcendent and mundane. It is unpresumptuous. It is empty of itself but can hold anything. It may feel both still and alive.

> *Gently turn awareness toward thinking — not the content of thoughts or the thinking process but the qualities of thinking itself. Do you notice any tension? If so, invite it to relax. See what happens.*

Micro-Gaps

Another way pure awareness of awareness arises is through noticing gaps in awareness. We usually think of awareness as an ever-changing stream of phenomena. But in reality, there are breaks when the flow is interrupted.

The most dramatic of these is dreamless sleep. We slumber unconsciously for as much as a third of each day. During these times, there is no awareness and nothing with which to identify. Without identification, there is no self. It's a mini-death: What we know ourselves to be vanishes. And it's perfectly safe. We do it every day.

There are other, more frequent micro-gaps in which thoughts disappear but awareness itself remains without content. For example, when we sneeze, thoughts, stories, and all the rest stop for a second. The next moment, they start up again. Without content or even discernible qualities, the mind has nothing to hold on to. So it barely notices the gap. It picks up where it left off without recognizing the break.

Yawning may also create a split-second break. Being startled can also do this. Something comes into awareness that is so novel that mental processing quits for a moment. Awareness is wide open, but there's no content or story, no processing, and no qualities. Then the processing starts up again: "What was that?"

Even more to the point are times when there are no distractions — no sneeze, no yawn, no startle — but content vanishes for a microsecond.

We blink an average of fifteen to twenty times a minute — more often than needed to keep the eyes moist. All totaled, our eyes are closed roughly 10 percent of our waking hours. Normally we don't notice it. But now that I've pointed it out, you may notice blinking for the next few minutes.

There are analogous gaps in our thinking. A thought arises, morphs, and fades. There is a microsecond — maybe less than a hundredth of a second — of pure, undistorted, empty awareness. Then the next thought arises.

As noted earlier, from the perspective of evolutionary selection, there is no advantage in noticing these gaps. So the mind stitches the end of the last thought to the beginning of the next without recognizing it jumped.

Micro-gaps are difficult to see only because it doesn't occur to us to watch for them. But just as we can become aware of eyeblinks, we can cultivate an awareness of thought-blinks.

To do this, we don't try to see the gaps — the effort of trying creates tension and distortion that encourages the mind to attend to the contents and processes rather than to the empty spaces. Rather than going into doing mode, we relax into receiving mode, which notices blank spots without trying to do anything with them.

For example, we can stop, close our eyes, relax, and notice thoughts arise and pass without trying to control them. If we do this with the lightest of effort, we may observe those tiny gaps between the cessation of one thought and the beginning of the next. It's a tiny moment of release. It's pleasant. And it's over so quickly that we usually ignore or dismiss it. But if we are open to receiving it, these gaps may bring a hint of a smile. Then they're gone. But sometimes the touch of well-being lingers.

> *Be receptive to micro-gaps. Notice if there is a tiny gap between the end of one thought and the beginning of the next. Don't search hard for it — you'll scare it away. But be gently receptive to noticing any tiny breaks in awareness.*

As we notice these micro-gaps, the mind learns to stop skipping over them so quickly. Those little fragments of well-being filter into conscious awareness. In our daily life when nothing is demanding our attention, we may even notice them as we walk around.

From Awareness of Awareness to Fading of Awareness

If we relax deeply enough, awareness starts to fade. It becomes dreamlike: We may wonder if we're asleep or awake or both. We seem to be noticing something, but we aren't sure what. In the text it's called "neither perception nor non-perception." We aren't fully perceiving. But we aren't exactly not perceiving either.

Perceiving requires a little tension — enough to identify what we are aware of. Memory also requires a little tension — enough to push the perception into memory banks. If, rather than tightening up to see what's going on, we just relax, then awareness may shut down completely. We stop perceiving and forming memories. I call this "winking out." We aren't aware of winking out at the time because there is no awareness.

When memory and perception come back on line, there is a blank spot in memory. We don't know what was going on a few moments before. It's as if we had nodded off. However, when we wake from sleep, the mind is usually fuzzy or groggy, whereas in this case, the mind is completely clear and lucid.

In the text, this winking out is called cessation (*nirodha*) — the cessation of perception, feeling, and consciousness.

If you're aware of awareness, relax the awareness itself.

From Fading Awareness to Nibbāna

If we wink out deeply enough, then when awareness returns, the mind is not only clear and lucid, it is luminous. Everything is fresh and different. We're so energized that we may not sleep for a few days. And the sense of self is gone. We see the interrelatedness of life as primary and the idea of a separate self as a convenient social convention, but nothing more.

These are the markers of nibbāna. Nibbāna is not an experience because there is no awareness. We recognize it only by the aftereffects: clarity, energy, and loss of a sense of a separate self.

We don't stay in nibbāna forever.

There is a story about the Tibetan saint Milarepa, who was traveling with a student. They stopped by the road to eat, laid out food, and closed their eyes to meditate for a few minutes before their meal.

When Milarepa opened his eyes, his student looked thin, tired, and bewildered. The food was dried up and mostly eaten by insects. Apparently Milarepa had been in nibbāna for a week, but hadn't noticed.

In nibbāna there is no experience. We don't even feel the passing of time. It is rare to be in nibbāna for long. Tension comes up and pulls us out. Unless we are a buddha or a Tibetan saint, it's unlikely that awareness will be off line for a long stretch. When awareness reemerges, it's helpful to gently look inside, see what pulled us back, and release it.

In the spectrum of awareness, we have gone up into nibbāna and come back down into the "Fading of Awareness." However, on the return trip, it might be called

"Emerging Awareness." There had been no awareness, and now there is. As before, it feels timeless and empty.

We can see why the Buddha called it "unborn awareness." We didn't create it or conjure it up. It seems to have been there — we just hadn't noticed it for a while. "Unborn" is not a metaphysical declaration but a phenomenological description. The Buddha was interested in describing experience as accurately as possible. "Unborn" is a good fit.

Jhānas and the Spectrum of Awareness

The Buddha talked about many styles of meditation. However, in the Theravada Buddhist text, the most common style by far is described in a series of *jhānas*. Jhānas are stages of consciousness that unfold in a specific manor.

Not coincidentally, the spectrum of awareness and the series of jhānas parallel and overlap. The spectrum is more detailed in the beginning stages while the jhānas are more nuanced in the subtle end of the spectrum.

If you are familiar with the jhānas, your familiarity may help you understand the spectrum. If you are unfamiliar with the jhānas or have difficulty getting into them, the spectrum may help guide your practice. The greatest challenge many meditators have with the jhānas is initially engaging them. The jhānas start with wholesome qualities — pretty far up on the spectrum. Engaging the early stages of the spectrum may offer an easier way to move into the jhānas.

In previous books,[5] I've gone into great detail about the jhānas, what they are, and how to cultivate them. I won't repeat that material here. But it may help to quickly review parallels between the jhānas and the subtle aspects of the spectrum of awareness.

The Buddha's map of the *jhānas* can be viewed as a systematic way of using micro-gaps as a tool for awakening.

The first jhāna is a brief, spontaneously arising joy or feeling of well-being that corresponds to the uplifted qualities in the spectrum. As our meditation deepens, these moments may appear without warning. A tiny upwelling of joy may cause us to smile quietly. This joy may have been triggered by a micro-gap that was too quick to be noticed consciously, but hung around long enough to create a moment of relief.

As we relax into that joy, it settles into happiness (the second jhāna); equanimity (the third jhāna); and deeper equanimity, in which body sensations fade into the background (the fourth jhāna).

As we relax into that peacefulness, the mind can feel quietly spacious (the fifth jhāna). As we spread out into the sense of limitlessness, we may notice periods where awareness is much stiller for a moment (the sixth jhāna). Awareness often will skip over that stillness. But if we let awareness go into the gap, the flow of awareness stops coalescing into a series of objects. There are no discrete things (the seventh jhāna). These are nuances of awareness of awareness.

---

[5] For example, *Buddha's Map* (2017).

As noted earlier, as we relax more deeply, awareness starts to break up into a dreamlike state that is neither perceiving nor non-perceiving (the eighth jhāna and fading of awareness). The eighth jhāna in turn fades into nirodha and nibbāna and non-awareness.

We can imagine moving gently through these jhānas or through this spectrum from the content of awareness up into nibbāna and back down. But in the real world, we rarely move smoothly up or down this road. We shift back and forth, leap from one place to another, or remain in several places at once. Resting in the waves means being open to all of it. It means welcoming the natural fluidity of experience.

We'll look at some of the practical ways to do this in the next few chapters.

Notice the fluidity of awareness. The body is always in flux (no two breaths are the same). The mind is always in flux (no two moments are the same). The qualities of the mind are always in flux (they never remain static). Awareness of awareness is fluid and always shifting.

5

Steadiness of Practice

In my early ventures into meditation, I wanted to know which "flavor" of Buddhism was best. Buddhism has three main branches from which I could select: Theravada, Mahayana, and Tibetan.

Theravada (Pāli for "school of the elders") is the oldest and most conservative branch. Geographically it is associated with Central and South Asia. It includes insight meditation (*vipassanā*) and awareness of breathing (*ānāpānasati*), among other practices. It looks to the extant records of the Buddha's talks (the suttas) as a primary source of inspiration and authenticity. And it offers commentary on these texts.

The Mahayana (Pāli for "great vehicle") grew out of Theravada as it migrated to East and Southeast Asia. It includes Zen and Pure Land Buddhism, among other schools. It promotes the *bodhisatta* ideal of reaching beyond monastic communities to the laity. It emphasizes that liberation can be achieved by anyone in this lifetime.

Tibetan Buddhism or Vajrayāna (Sanskrit for "diamond vehicle" or "thunderbolt vehicle") grew out of Mahayana Buddhism over a thousand years after the Buddha died. It blended with some elements of the native Tibetan Bon religion with its special powers, rites, and rituals. Today Tibetan Buddhism retains a wide and rich array of practices.

In my early years of practice, I did some training in all three. Each branch has its characteristic flavor.

I found I was more drawn to Theravada. In time I realized that this was not because it was necessarily best for everyone, it's that it just suited me. All three branches have produced many wise and clear beings.

The Buddha taught different practices to different people. Looking through the ancient records, it's clear he was talented in assessing individuals' gifts and vulnerabilities and suggesting a well-matched path.

There is no need to find a winning team in the Buddhist Super Bowl. We only have to find a good-enough path for ourselves and those who seek our guidance. The path will be a little different for each of us.

Having said that, there are common themes in all three branches and in all the Buddha's practices. This chapter explores some of those common elements and the steadiness of the practice. In the next chapter, we'll look at its fluidity.

Taking Time

The first prerequisite for any spiritual practice is time. With the pace of modern life, this can seem difficult. But the heart of spiritual practice is helping the mind-heart rediscover its nature. As the musician David Darling put it, "Nothing is difficult. Some things take time." Spiritual practices take time and patience.

A Vedic text says, "Truth waits for eyes unclouded by longing." Wisdom arises naturally when awareness is patient, relaxed, clear, open, receptive, and not fogged by emotion. Usually it's not.

As I write these words, the sky outside my window is overcast. There is a clear sky above the clouds, but not down here where I am. We can't create a clear mind any more than we can create a clear sky — it's already there. But we can clear some of the cloud cover of reactivity.

As we saw earlier, evolution gave us neural systems that grabs our attention by creating clouds of emotions: fear, anger, delight, longing, etc. We can't turn the signal system off. But we can set aside times when there are fewer triggers. In daily meditation or on retreats we can do what's reasonable to reduce disturbances and distractions. We can simplify the environment for an hour of meditation or several weeks of retreat. Taking time on a regular basis is a vital part of any spiritual practice and deep living.

This helps us find moments of "eyes unclouded by longing." They remind us of what's possible as they expose the clear awareness beyond the overcast sky. It can be such a relief that we just want more.

But the clouds return again and again. With time and practice, we become less interested in getting rid of the clouds and more interested in what keeps bringing them back. If we can deal with the causes, there will be fewer clouds.

> *How much time do you give to meditation? When you practice, what do you long for? How much of your practice is motivated by longing? How much by pushing? How much by being?*

Attuning, not Attaining

As our meditation practice deepens and steadies, we see that spiritual awakening is not about attaining. It is about attuning. Attuning requires time, patience, and seeing clearly.

The Buddha taught the primacy of awareness. Spiritual deepening is not the result of behavior, rites, rituals, social status, beliefs, or philosophical conclusions. It is the result of seeing clearly and directly how life actually works. It is the result of awareness.

One Pāli word for this is *vipassanā.* The term is usually translated as "insight," but literally means "clear seeing" or "clear knowing."

Just as twentieth-century Western psychologist came to understand, the Buddha recognized that knowing begins with contact between the organism and the environment. It begins with the phenomenon of awareness. In a sense, they were all phenomenologists.

If awareness is the by-product of our physiology and neural networks, then to have greater awareness, we would have to train ourselves and our brains to manufacture deeper and clearer states. But if awareness is a primary property of the universe, then we can't train it. However, we can attune to what's already here.

Meditation is not about creating something new, it's about revealing something that's been hidden. It's not about doing, it's about being. It's not about giving birth to something novel, but about recognizing something that's been here all along. We want to listen more than create, surrender more than control, receive more than act, and attune more than attain.

The amount of attuning that the mind needs depends on the clarity it already has.

Awakened awareness is clear, open, present, softly luminous, peaceful, and responsive to the world without being reactive. Truly awakened people don't need formal meditation because their normal state is the same as deep meditative awareness.

On the other hand, overcast awareness is opaque, dense, lost in the past or future, unresponsive, and reactive. Such people are lost and out of touch. Meditation might be helpful, but they're unlikely to engage spiritual practice because they're too absent to know there's a problem.

Most of us are somewhere between these extremes. We have moments of clear, unfettered awareness and moments of opacity and irritability. But we recognize there's a problem and that meditation training might be beneficial.

Some of us know our minds go out of balance and that the essence of the problem is tension. Others know there is a problem but don't know its source. They know they are discontented but don't really understand how to work with it. This can be painful and discouraging. It happens often with new meditators, who have not yet learned how to work effectively with the tension and tightness in the mind or even that that is the root of their difficulty.

> *When distractions arise in the mind, what are some of the typical ways you respond? How much do you see it as a helpful reminder to relax? How much do you get caught in the content?*

Home Base

To work with our difficulty and attune, the mind needs a job. If we leave it unchaperoned without anything to do, it wanders off into the wilderness or gets caught in a briar patch. It picks through old conversations, makes shopping lists, drifts into fantasies, anticipates, explains, worries, fogs up, and more.

Most styles of meditation start by choosing a home base and giving the mind the job of returning to it when it rambles off. The home base could be the breath, a mantra, kindness, a kōan, or almost anything. The main difference between different styles of meditation is what home base they recommend.

Awareness of the breath is a popular home base because it's easy to use in the beginning and directly addresses the concern of most beginning meditators: "What do I do with the herd of buffalo stampeding through my mind?"

Focusing on the sensations of the breath draws attention out of the mental dust. Thoughts can be about the past or future. But body sensations are in the present and are easy to find.

The limitation of using the breath as a home base, as it is commonly used, is that it focuses on the coarse end of the spectrum of awareness. Meditation is ultimately about the *qualities* of awareness, not the *content* of awareness. Putting too much attention on physical sensations can bog us down in content. I used the breath for twenty-five years. I made good progress in the beginning, but ultimately my practice plateaued.

Mettā meditation begins with uplifted qualities. When I shifted to that home base, my practice accelerated and went to places I had not imagined possible. In the beginning, mettā can be difficult because mental qualities are subtle and can be hard to see. However, we all know what kindness, compassion, joy, and equanimity feel like, even if we aren't feeling them in a given moment. If we lightly send out mettā or well-wishing, uplifted qualities gradually take hold.

> *What's your home base? How fresh is it? How stale? How alive?*

Steadiness

In many meditation styles, as the practice deepens, the home base shifts from coarser to subtler qualities. The home base can be fluid. So we'll come back to this in the next chapter when we talk about the fluidity of practice. But having a home base of some kind is part of the steadiness of practice.

It doesn't help to jump quickly from one home base to another — it's better to find a good one and let it settle in for a while. The middle way is neither jumping around too much nor doggedly staying in one place.

Whatever we use for a home base, it's helpful that it be farther up the spectrum of awareness than where our mind normally rests. Otherwise, it doesn't serve as well as it could.

No matter what home base we use, the mind still sneaks out the back door and wanders off over and over again. Having a base doesn't really solve our problem — it just makes it more obvious. We become painfully aware of how out of control the mind is. It can be frustrating and discouraging.

This may have been the Buddha's point. He said often that he was concerned with only one thing: suffering and the relief from suffering. It sounds like two things!

I think what he meant was that his main concern was relieving suffering. But we can't find a cure if we don't know there is a disease. So the use of a home base often flushes hidden discomfort to the surface.

Three Essential Practices

Most students and scholars agree that the root of the Buddha's teachings is the so-called Four Noble Truths (*cattāri ariyasaccāni* in Pāli). They are the bedrock of all Buddhist practice in all three branches: Theravada, Mahayana, and Vajrayāna.

I say "so-called" because they aren't philosophical or metaphysical truths. They are pedestrian observations about life. *Noble* doesn't refer to the observations. The Pāli term is idiomatic — "noble" refers to the mind that sees clearly. The Buddhist scholar Stephen Batchelor refers to them as the "Four Ennobling Truths" — they ennoble us when we work with them wisely.

Each observation has a verb — a practice — to help us attune more deeply. They are meditation instructions. There are only three practices. The supposed fourth is the "Eightfold Path" — a kind of eightfold checklist. If the first three practices are not working well, the eight are areas we can check to better attune our meditation.

Turning Toward

The first essential practice is turning toward whatever experience arises.

The first Ennobling Truth is called *dukkha*, a Pāli term for "suffering" or "dissatisfaction." The Buddha doesn't say that life *is* suffering, only that it *has* discomfort. The practice of returning our awareness to a home base helps us see how difficult such a simple task can be. In pointing this out, the Buddha is saying to us, "It's not your fault. You aren't to blame. Don't take the discomfort personally or think you're doing something wrong. It's just what happens in this world."

Rather than blame ourselves for hurting, the Buddha says, "suffering is to be understood." "Understanding" is a practice we engage. This does not mean analyzing. When a friend understands us, she knows how we think, how we feel, what lifts us up, what gets us down, what makes us tick. The Buddha says we need to understand intimately how suffering and dissatisfaction work.

We can't do this if we are busy pushing the angst away, trying to rise above it, or straining to control it. Instead we simply turn toward whatever we experience. We don't try to push it away or fix it — just see it as it is.

> *How welcoming are you in turning toward your inner experience? How often do you turn away?*

Relaxing Into

The second essential practice is "relaxing into."

When we understand dukkha, we see that it's rooted in tension (Pāli: *taṇhā*). The practice associated with taṇhā sounds dramatic: "taṇhā is to be abandoned." To abandon tension, we relax. Rather than relax to get away from it or just grinning and bearing it, we relax into it.

Anytime the mind is distracted in meditation or elsewhere, tension is a contributing cause. The tension may be thick and obvious or subtle and hard to see. Tension also contributes to a sense of solidity in the mind and to a sense of self. Tightness disrupts the natural flux and flow of experience.

There is an evolutionary survival advantage to being sensitive to threats. Tension stimulates thinking. So when the mind wanders a lot, it's helpful to notice if something truly does need attention — we left the water running, someone is knocking at the door, a wasp landed on our hand. If so, it may be best to attend to it. But if it is a false alarm, we reassure the mind and relax.

It's important to give the reassurance and relax the tension rather than power through it or ignore it.

> *How easily do you relax into tension? How often do you push it away or hold on to it?*

Deepening or Savoring

The third essential practice takes this a step further. It says it is not enough to see superficially what's going on. It helps to see into the core of it. We need to see deeply what's going on underneath our experience.

So, for example, if we turn toward and relax into our fear, hurt, or heartache, we see tenderness underneath. If we weren't tender — if we were an emotional brick — we wouldn't suffer. Anytime there is discomfort, there has to be some tenderness beneath it.

If we relax into this tenderness, we may notice openness or spaciousness. Without these, there would be no tenderness.

If we relax into the openness, we may experience freedom.

We want that sense of freedom, inner peace, spiritual aliveness, openness of being. Too often we look for it by turning away from difficulty, hardening against hurt, or distracting ourselves. But the only path that works in the long run goes *through* the suffering and tenderness rather than *around* them.

Of course, when we turn toward and relax into our experience, there is not always pain or suffering. Sometimes there is peacefulness, ease, or well-being. Deepening into these feels like savoring.

The third essential practice implicitly recognizes that we are more sensitive to negative experiences than to positive ones. Neuroscientists say we are four times more likely to notice pain than pleasure. So when an uplifted feeling arises, the Buddha said it should be "realized," as in "making it real." We not only welcome it, we let it soak in. We savor it. This allows it to deepen.

The three essential practices could be summarized as "welcoming": We turn toward whatever arises, relax into it, and deepen or savor it.

> *Can you deepen through the "difficult stuff" without turning away? Can you savor the "good stuff" without getting lost in it?*

Wise Effort

Turning toward, relaxing into, and deepening are an overview of Buddhist meditation practice.

However, the most difficult part of meditation is dealing wisely with hindrances. Hindrances are distractions that grab our attention. They are unwelcome intruders. It may take effort to get the practice back on track. So it's easy to use too much effort — strain to get rid of strain, get uptight over tightness, or confused about what to do with confusion.

If we just push awareness back to the home base, the pushing adds tension to tension. The tension makes the mind restless — it wanders off again and again. We're at risk of sliding into a discouraging downward spiral.

Wise effort, in contrast, means effort without strain. This is so important that one of my teachers, Bhante Vimalaraṁsi, and his students put together a simple, paint-by-numbers implementation of what the Buddha meant by "wise effort." It's called the Six Rs: *Recognize, Release, Relax, Re-smile, Return,* and *Repeat.* The Rs are both tangible enough to use anywhere along the path and flexible enough to work in most situations. And they are self-correcting.

They can be used across a wide variety of home bases and depths of practice because they are primarily concerned with skillfully releasing tension. Tension will change and get subtler as meditation deepens. But tension will be there in some form.

The Six Rs are used when the mind wanders off while meditating. At first there is nothing we can do about it. We're lost in thought and don't even notice — we're no longer attending. But at some point, wisdom brings us back to the present, often accompanied by an observation such as, "Oh, I'm supposed to be meditating." How do we get back to the meditation practice at this point?

The answer is "Six-R": *Recognize, Release, Relax, Re-smile, Return, Repeat.*

Recognize

The first *R*, Recognize, is part of turning toward. We recognize where the mind is at that moment. Thought content is not helpful. It is more useful to notice the processes in the mind: thinking, worrying, planning, and so on. If the qualities of awareness are easily seen, we can recognize them as well.

Release

The second *R*, Release, is also part of turning toward. To help us recognize clearly, we release what we see by just letting things be as they are without holding on to them or pushing them away. We mentally step back to get a wider view.

Relax

The third step is to Relax or "relax into." It's the second essential practice and the most important of the Rs.

Tension (taṇhā) is a common element in all distractions. Sometimes the tension is thick and obvious. Sometimes it is subtle and hard to see. But any time the mind wanders, there will be some level of tension. Otherwise the mind-heart would be serene and steady.

Recognize

Release

Relax

Re-Smile

Return

Repeat

Tension is also the glue that holds the sense of self together and the clouds that obscure natural unborn awareness. So relaxing helps loosen up the density of selfhood and lightens awareness at the same time.

We can't force relaxation! Trying to do so is counterproductive. We just invite the body, emotions, and mind to soften or relax.

When asked how to become enlightened, the Buddhist teacher Adyashanti said, "Relax."

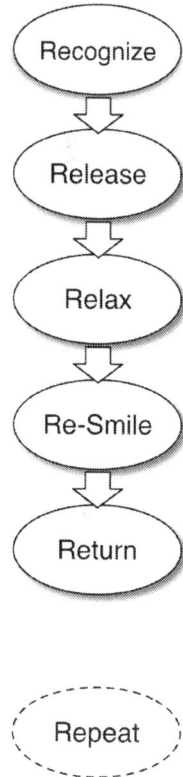

Re-Smile

The fourth step is to smile. We call it "Re-smile" because we need an *R* word and because we'll be doing this a lot.

When the tension drains, it leaves an open space in the mind-heart. Old habits can rush in to fill the void. So we deliberately invite uplifted qualities like kindness, compassion, or peacefulness to pervade that spaciousness. But we don't force anything. If no uplifted qualities arise easily, we lift the corners of the mouth in a quiet smile. Because of brain wiring, mechanically smiling can trigger a gentle feeling of uplift without pushing.

Re-smiling is part of the third essential practice: deepening or savoring.

Return

The fifth *R* is to Return to our regular meditation practice, which might be sending out mettā, observing the breath, or another kind of meditation practice. We return to our home base. If our home base is sending out uplifted qualities, this *R* becomes part of the essential practice of deepening.

Repeat

The final *R* is Repeat. Anytime the mind gets lost, we repeat the Rs. The repeat step is a reminder that we will be doing the Six Rs a lot and that patience is helpful in any spiritual discipline. With patience, practice is so much easier and more enjoyable.

Rolling the Rs

As we practice the Six Rs, they tend to flow together. This can be helpful. We call it "rolling the *R*s." We could also call it "welcoming" because that's how the *R*s feel as they merge into a single motion.

As they blend together, sometimes one of the *R*s fades without us noticing. So it's helpful to take them in for a tune-up from time to time: Intentionally slow them down into the six separate movements. That way we'll see quickly if all six are still there or not. If one has faded, we bring it back. Once they are all going, we let them roll back into a single flow of welcoming.

Having a steady home base to return to and cultivating an ease in using the Six Rs help the mind stabilize. They keep the mind from running all over the place. And when it does, they give it a way for settling down into a steady practice that opens the mind-heart. And this, in turn, builds wisdom by helping us see *how* the mind-heart works.

However, it's not helpful for the mind to get too stiff and thick. The awakened mind-heart has a natural ease and flow, which is the topic of the next chapter.

6

Fluidity of Practice

"Taming the mind is like taming a wild elephant," the teacher explained. I sat toward the back of the meditation hall at the Insight Meditation Society in Barre, Massachusetts. It was June 1974 and I was starting my first extended meditation retreat.

She continued, "In ancient India, an elephant trainer secured one end of a chain to the leg of the beast and the other end to a post pounded deep into the ground. At first, the elephant was mellow. But when it realized it was tethered, it rebelled, tugged, and flailed. But it couldn't break free — fighting was futile. Eventually the elephant wore out, accepted the situation, and settled down."

The teacher paused to let the image sink in. Then she said, "Chain your awareness to the breath. Your mind will run off into stories, thoughts, images, and ideas. Bring your attention back to the breath over and over. It will gradually accept that breathing is here to stay and settle into it."

At the time, I found the metaphor persuasive and did my best to practice as she suggested. Sometimes the cycles of rebellion and calm were not pretty. However, the quiet moments gradually lengthened. The strategy worked.

While I was grateful, I was not totally satisfied: Treating the mind like a rogue elephant was not the same as welcoming.

In the following years, I came back for more retreats with similar instructions. But I was curious to know more about what was really going on in the rogue mind. So when attention wandered, I didn't always reign it in. Sometimes I took it to heart, the way I might embrace a rambunctious child. When I did this, the mind seemed to have more energy than it knew what to do with. It was trying to burn off excess vim. Going from object to object, story to story, and topic to topic dispersed superfluous energy. This was not particularly skillful or effective. But I saw that the mind wasn't being "naughty." It was doing the best it could with what it already knew.

> *How do you feel toward the mind when it wanders off without asking permission? If you can't control it, whose mind is it anyway?*

As I became more adept, I noticed times when the mind was *not* chaotic. This quiet had always been there, obscured by the noise. Now I was becoming more aware of it.

At these times, foremost in awareness was not a series of objects but a series of processes. Sometimes the mind just muttered. Sometimes it explained. Sometimes it argued, whined, daydreamed, planned, or plotted.

These activities had content. But I could see the processes apart from their content: I noticed explaining apart from the explanations, worrying apart from what I worried about, excitement apart from what was exciting.

I was beginning to understand that the types of things the mind can notice vary over a wide spectrum (pp. 63–75).

Sometimes the best I could do was to see the chaos in the mind. Sometimes I could see individual objects within the cacophony. Sometimes I could see subtler processes behind the various objects. Sometimes I could see the qualities of awareness that gave birth to those processes. Sometimes I could see awareness itself, without which I wouldn't have known any of this.

I was beginning to suspect that the practices that deepen awareness necessarily vary. When the mind is chaotic, it is difficult and discouraging to try to see the mental processes themselves. On the other hand, when awareness is subtle, bringing attention back to a single, coarse object such as the breath can actually prevent awareness from becoming serene.

Fluidity helps the practice adapt wisely.

No Best Home Base

Years ago I could not have imagined writing that last sentence. I knew there were different styles of meditation: "different strokes for different folks." But I assumed one home base was better than others. I was searching for the most effective technique so I could master it.

But a single, optimal technique doesn't exist. The best practice is contextual. The most effective ways to meditate are as fluid as the mind.

If this leaves us feeling like Wile E. Coyote suspended in midair, then it helps to welcome that feeling as well. To let our practice evolve, we have to relax into its fluidity. The moment itself becomes our teacher.

Just because there are times when our practice is subtle and refined enough to be aware of awareness doesn't mean that that will be our optimal home base from now on. The next time we meditate, the mind may be a wild elephant.

And just because the elephant flailed the last time doesn't preclude the possibility that our next meditation may drop into deep stillness.

As noted before, the mind has a mind of its own. We are navigators, not pilots. It is best to welcome surprise. The more we welcome the mind's fluidity no matter what's going on, the more receptive we are to the deep stillness and contentment that float behind all awareness.

Corruption vs. Ignorance

My early forays into Buddhist practice touched on basic questions about human nature, though I didn't appreciate it at the time. The orthodox Christian view is that humans are fundamentally corrupt — "original sin." We are not capable of the deepest happiness without the intervention of outside forces, such as God.

A modern agnostic view leaves divinity out of the equation but assumes our core nature is more like a feral elephant than a serene buddha. It replaces an external God with internal willpower. We need some force — such as meditative discipline — to shape us up. It may not be easy ("no pain, no gain"), but we need to save ourselves from our wayward tendencies. This attitude suggests forceful and disciplined spiritual practices.

Awareness, not Will

The Buddha's view of human nature was different. He suggested we are fundamentally noble — original goodness. We already have what we need for the deepest contentment and well-being. Our problem is not corruption, it is ignorance: We don't fully recognize our Buddha nature. So spiritual practice is less about fixing us and more about seeing clearly what we truly are already. It's not about beliefs, rituals, concepts, philosophies, or metaphysics. It is about penetrating mindfulness. When awareness is deep enough, we know effortlessly what to do and what not to do. Meditation is less about willpower and more about sensitive wakefulness.

Open, clear awareness is alive and fluid. If we pay attention, no two sittings are exactly the same. Similarly, optimal meditation techniques are fluid and able to adapt to what we see and learn.

The Buddha taught different people in different ways. He recognized that different people had different gifts and blind spots, and he offered techniques best suited to them.

He also expected that the techniques a person used would have to adapt and change as the person progressed. He didn't teach "one size fits all" or even that one technique fits a given person all the time."

Fluidity of the Jhānas

The most striking illustration of the Buddha's fluidity of practice is the jhānas.

The jhānas describe eight stages of practice, each with characteristic qualities. The insights gained in each jhāna suggest how a meditator can shift their practice. It's a bootstrapping in which insights from one phase make deeper, subtler techniques available for the next phase.[6]

---

[6] In *Buddha's Map* (2017) I describe these stages in detail as well as how to adapt meditation techniques to take advantage of each.

The jhānas proceed through joy, happiness, peacefulness, spaciousness, stillness, fading of distinct objects into a sense of flow, and the fading of perception itself. The Buddha's map does not use a never-changing home base. To be sure, the base doesn't jump around chaotically. But neither is awareness chained to a single object. Instead it slowly and gracefully shifts to subtler and subtler objects as our practice deepens.

> *How do you decide when to let the mind-heart find its own way and when to assert meditative discipline? When is the use of willpower helpful? When is awareness alone enough?*

Breath

A shifting home base was not how I was taught when I began Buddhist practice. My early teachers relied heavily on one home base: the breath. It is ubiquitous in many American Insight practices as well as in stress reduction programs in the larger community.

But when Bhante Vimalaraṁsi encouraged me to read what the Buddha said about meditation, I realized there were only a few texts that referred to breath-based awareness, whereas about a third of the texts mention jhānas.

And even breath awareness does not stay exclusively on the breath. The *Ānāpānasati Sutta* (*Discourse on Mindfulness of Breathing*) has the most detail about the breath as a meditation home base. It starts with knowing the sensations of the breath — long or short, coarse or subtle, and so on. As we settle into those sensations, attention shifts from single breaths to awareness of breathing throughout the whole body. Then it shifts from the body to joy. From there it progresses up through the jhānas. The breath sensations are only used as an entry point into deeper jhāna practice.

Four Ingredients

The jhānas parallel the spectrum of awareness described in chapter 4. The difference is that jhāna practice lumps together the whole lower end of the spectrum. Everything before uplifted qualities is treated as a distraction to be Six-R'ed. On the other hand, the jhānas start with uplifted qualities at the upper end of the spectrum — joy, happiness, and peace — and go up from there. Since all of us have some familiarity with these refined places, we are able to use them.

However, for those who are new to meditation, or do not meditate regularly, the first step from everyday awareness to uplifted qualities can be daunting. In these cases I've found the framework of the Four Ingredients of the mind can be a helpful bridge. To review, the ingredients are

1. The world around us
2. Wired-in proclivities
3. Personal history
4. Willpower

Here's an example of what this can look like in everyday life:

One summer a construction project began next to the home of a friend of mine in Sacramento. The project went on for months. Because of the summer heat in Central California, the workers started at dawn when it was relatively cool so they could get in a full day's work before the temperature climbed through the nineties.

My friend liked to meditate in the early morning. The workers used large machines equipped with alarms that beeped a tone and timbre that drew attention. It was unpleasant.

At first, he Six-R'ed these alarm sounds. But as the days and weeks rolled by, he found he was bracing himself for the beeps before they started.

He spoke with the workers. They were sympathetic. They noted that they did not use jackhammers or other loud equipment before normal work hours. But to get anything done, they needed to move their equipment. If they disabled those backup alarms, they'd get cited for a safety violation.

His meditation and quality of life degenerated. He used the Six Rs, but they were not enough. So I encouraged him to stay longer with the first of the Six Rs: *Recognize*. Together we identified the various ingredients of his experience.

1. *The World Around Us.* The most obvious was the environment — the beeping. He did what he could externally to stop it, but it continued. Unconsciously, he tried to shut it out of his mind. But the body is designed to notice threat signals. Trying to use willpower to blank out an alarm was futile and exhausting.

2. *Wired-in Proclivities.* The biological ingredient was less obvious because, under stress, the mind looks "out there" rather than "in here." However, with a few prompts, he recognized the sound itself, apart from his feelings about it, and that, in itself, it was neutral. Nevertheless, he noticed, the mind found the sound uncomfortable; it tightened up and labeled the whole thing an "awful problem." He couldn't prevent these reactions. They were wired-in.

3. *Personal History.* The personal-history ingredient of the mind had developed as the days and weeks rolled by and he began to anticipate the disturbance, at which point, he tried

to solve the "awful problem." When he couldn't, the mind slumped into discouragement.

4. *Willpower.* The willpower ingredient resided in his attempt to make the problem go away. However, willpower is not very strong when compared with the forces of the world around us, wired-in proclivities, and personal history. Not knowing what else to do, he tried to just will it all away. The task was too much.

The Buddha's awakening and the core of his teaching was based on an analysis of phenomena such as these, which he called the Links of Dependent Origination.[7] The primary sound that so disturbed my friend would be identified by the Buddha as simply a body-based sensation (*phassa*). The discomfort would be a feeling tone (*vedanā*). The tension was *taṇhā*, which we've spoke of earlier in the book. The label "awful problem" was clinging (*upādāna*). The attempt to figure out a solution was a habitual tendency (*bhava*). The attempt to implement the solution was an action (*jāti*). And the discouragement was suffering (*jarāmaraṇa*).

I thought that trying to teach him these finer points of the Links of Dependent Origination while in the midst of a crisis would not be kind or effective. But the Four Ingredients could provide a simpler strategy to help him untangle his situation. The most important elements were the beeping sound (which was impersonal and out of his control), the inner tightening (which was an impersonal reflex and out of his control), and the discouragement (which was a natural response to a seemingly intransigent situation).

---

[7] Kraft, *Buddha's Map* (2017), chap. 4, "Thickening the Plot," describes these links in detail.

Using this simplified model, he could redirect his precious resources of effort and will from the large and nearly impossible job of shutting down the whole chain of events. Instead we focused his effort on one aikido-like move: relaxing the tension. We can't always do this completely: Sometimes the tension is a physiological response. But we can invite relaxation.

That was enough to get him onto a reasonable and doable path. He wasn't wasting willpower on things over which he had little or no control.

Conserving Effort Wisely

The story illustrates an important aspect of the Buddha's practice: conserving effort for when we need it most.

Awareness is more important than willpower. When we see what's going on clearly enough, we naturally know what to do and what not to do. We shouldn't waste our precious will on trying to control the world around us or within us. It's better to use gentle intention to cultivate open, clear, agenda-less awareness.

Relaxing tension is key to clear awareness and fluid meditation practice as well as to expansive and joyful living. Compared with ancient India, modern Western culture puts more emphasis on controlling than on relaxing, on being the master of our fate than on being curious about what life is offering, and on being on top of our game rather than surrendering to the moment. Without our science, technology, and gadgetry, ancient yogis were less likely to think they should be the captains of their ships.

The Buddha was speaking to his contemporaries. He had no understanding of our modern cultural biases. So we have to look a little deeper into his teachings to realize things that were obvious to his people but not to us.

Agenda-less Awareness of Awareness

When we look deeper into the Buddha's teachings, we see how his practice conserves effort by emphasizing awareness. Agenda-less awareness is inherently calming. This peacefulness deepens our motivation.

Meditation master Sayadaw U Tejaniya puts it this way: "If awareness never comes off the object of awareness and onto awareness itself, your practice will not go very far."

Awareness of awareness is subtle. However, cultivating a kind openness toward awareness requires less willpower than manipulating its content. So in the long run, it's more effective.

For example, I look out the window in the morning and see it's cold and rainy. Before I go out, I slip on a jacket and pick up an umbrella. When I see the weather, I know what to do and what not to do. I don't need a set of rules that say

- Wear a jacket when it's cold.
- Don't wear a jacket when it's warm.
- Take an umbrella if it's raining or looks like it could rain.
- Leave the umbrella at home if the sky is clear.

If I had to go through that checklist every day, it would take longer to get going and life would feel stiff and regimented. The Buddha, in contrast, put more faith in awareness than in willpower. It made life simpler and more joyful.

To be sure, the monks had lots of rules. But precepts were not intended to bludgeon someone into line. They were tools of awareness. For example, a monk takes a precept to refrain from lying and harming. If he's tempted to lie or hurt someone, the precept reminds him to slow down and pay more attention to what's going on inside. The monks had the faith that when they truly saw what's going on, they'd know instinctively what to do and what not to do.

Awareness Can Be Bad News, Too

Even when awareness is strong, we still need some willpower because awareness is often bad news. Sometimes it takes a little effort to stay with experience and Six-R it rather than reflexively push unpleasantness aside.

Ram Dass tells a tale about how this works:

The rabbi knelt down at the altar and began to beat his chest and intone, "I'm nobody, I'm nobody, I'm nobody."

The cantor bent his knees next to the rabbi, beat his chest, and lamented, "I'm nobody, I'm nobody, I'm nobody."

The janitor knelt next to the cantor, beat his chest, and moaned, "I'm nobody, I'm nobody, I'm nobody."

The cantor turned to the rabbi and said, "Look who thinks he's nobody."

We can imagine the cantor's many thoughts and feelings: pride in his humility, caring for the suffering of some people, disdain for the janitor, protectiveness of sacred rituals, self-doubt, high-mindedness, low-mindedness, longing to be appreciated, and more.

He probably wasn't conscious of all of these. But like the moon below the horizon pulling the tides, unseen thoughts and feelings would have had a gravitational effect on the cantor's mood, speech, and actions.

Like the cantor, we all have a lot going on inside. We're conscious of some things and oblivious of others. With billions of neurons in the brain, multiple circuits are usually active at the same time. If we were fully aware of all of them, we'd be overwhelmed. So the mind filters awareness: Some things surface, while others hover below the horizon.

One mental filter is self-image. Things that support our self-concept are easier to notice than things that conflict with it. The cantor found it easier to see his humility than his pride, his caring than his disdain, his confidence than his self-doubt. The same is true for us: It's easier to notice what harmonizes with our self-sense than the things that are discordant with it.

In the short run, self-awareness is often bad news: Things that emerge from the depths are often the things we once pushed down because they were disturbing, harmful, or didn't support our self-image.

But there is no freedom outside of truth. Repressed feelings affect us. So seeing them all is helpful, even if they are uncomfortable for a while. Learning to tolerate uncomfortable feelings is a boon in the long run. It's said that "pain is inevitable, suffering is optional."

Dependent Origination

Another example of conserving willpower wisely can be found in the Links of Dependent Origination or Dependent Co-Arising (*paṭiccasamuppāda*), which we explored earlier in this chapter. It shows how willpower can be conserved by one's cultivating subtler and subtler awareness.

Dependent Origination says that everything arises out of causes and conditions. And those causes and conditions arise out of subtler antecedents in a chain of causality.

Resting in the Waves

It's like a line of dominoes: As each one falls forward, it knocks down the one in front of it. However, in the Links of Dependent Origination, each domino is slightly larger than the one behind that knocked it over. So the force and momentum increase the farther we go down the line. It takes more and more effort and willpower to stop the larger dominoes from tipping over.

For example, the smell of fresh bread is just an aroma. But it can trigger a bigger "domino": pleasantness. Pleasantness can trigger attraction. Attraction has more momentum and tension than the aroma alone. It can trigger craving, which can trigger the thought "I want a bite of that," which can trigger thoughts about how to get that bread, which can trigger the action of getting the bread. And so forth. As we go down the causal chain, the dominoes get bigger, have more momentum and tension, and are harder to stop.

However, as awareness gets subtler, we can see and intervene earlier in the chain. With careful observation, we can use this causal chain to our advantage. Rather than wrestling with the gross effects at the end of the chain, we look for and relax the subtler causes within causes. This requires some effort and patience. But it's easier because the smaller dominoes require less effort. As we see smaller antecedents, awareness itself becomes enough to stop the chain reaction.[8]

---

[8] Kraft, *Buddha's Map* (2017) goes into more detail on Dependent Origination.

Noticing the Mind's Tone of Voice

A simple practice that is an offshoot of Dependent Origination is noticing the tone of voice that is speaking in the mind. This can be very helpful with a busy mind. Rather than attending to what the mind is saying, we attend to the quality and volume of the voice that is speaking. For example, ask yourself whether the voice sounds loud, grumpy, edgy, curious, or submissive? This is a way to step out of the topic in the mind without pushing it away.

We may think the content of the mind determines the tone of the mind. But the opposite is usually true: The subtle tone generates the coarser content.

For example, if the mind is arguing as we try to meditate, it's easy to get involved in the content — who's right and who's wrong and why. It seems like the content is important and stirring up trouble; however, if we resolve the argument, the mind often picks another fight. In other words, the arguing comes first, the content second.

What is most helpful is seeing the arguing as a process unto itself and Six-R'ing and relaxing the tension in the process. With this, the content tends to evaporate as irrelevant.

Habit

Another way to rely less on willpower is to cultivate wholesome habits. It's said that habit is stronger than will. A modest amount of effort is needed to develop a habit. But as the habit grows, less willpower is required to maintain it.

It's as if we're trying to traverse a meadow of waist-high grass. The first time through requires a lot of effort. The tenth time takes less exertion because we've started to wear down a path. The hundredth time is easy because the well-worn track offers little resistance. It still takes some intention to follow the path. However we can glide down it with relative ease.

Similarly, to develop a meditation practice it helps to practice every day. This way we rely more on the momentum of habit and less on brute will. I recommend yogis sitting thirty to four-five minutes minimum in the beginning. However, if you can't find the time on any given day, it helps to sit as much as you can, even if it's only five minutes. This builds a daily habit.

Another habit is to sit regularly with a group of meditators. It's easier to sit in a group than alone because the group support means we utilize less force of will. And at the same time, we're deepening the habit of sitting regularly.

Ancillary Practices

Even when our overall meditation strategy is fluid and we are conserving willpower effectively, there are times when the mind-heart gets stuck or stale anyway. We may not need to overhaul our practice. But some short-term intervention may be helpful.

There are many practices and techniques to help intervene. Most of these ancillary practices can be employed for a while, then allowed to fade unless or until they are needed again. The following are a sampling of practices we might consider fluidly as needed: forgiveness, empirical trials, asking "What else?", nondual awareness, moving toward the present, and being in multiple places.

Forgiveness

When meditation practice gets stuck, one way to loosen it up is to switch to forgiveness meditation.[9] Forgiveness is particularly helpful when we identify with negative feelings or experiences.

Forgiveness heals by welcoming whatever is going on without trying to control anything. It uses phrases similar to the beginning mettā practice, but the phrases center on forgiving. We can make up our own or use the following traditional four. At first, we focus on ourselves:

I forgive myself for not understanding.

I forgive myself for making mistakes.

I forgive myself for harming myself or someone else.

I forgive myself for not following my own sense of what's right.

We repeat a phrase or two slowly until we feel it. We radiate that feeling of welcoming acceptance to ourselves. If the mind resists, we gently Six-R the resistance and come back to forgiving ourselves.

The mind may naturally go to a person who left us or hurt us in some way. If so, we direct forgiveness to that person:

I forgive you for not understanding.

I forgive you for making mistakes.

I forgive you for harming yourself or someone else.

I forgive you for not following my sense of what's right.

We don't get involved in the story line — that doesn't help. We just repeat whatever phrases seem best until we feel

---

[9] See Kraft, *Buddha's Map* (2017); *Meditator's Field Guide* (2018), and on the Web at www.easingawake.com by going to the "Forgiveness collection" on the "Talks/Articles" menu.

them. When the mind becomes distracted, we gently Six-R and start again.

The mind may naturally go to someone we hurt or abandoned. If we feel remorse, guilt, or regret, we shift the practice again. We imagine them looking at us and hear them saying, "I forgive you for _____. I truly do forgive you." We allow that feeling to soak in.

If we get stuck and are unable to forgive or feel forgiving, that may mean that we have a subtle attachment or aversion to anger, guilt, or allowing ourselves to be forgiven. This holding on or pushing away can be forgiven and released as well.

We can take this practice into the rest of our life by forgiving everything. We forgive ourselves for knocking something over, spilling something, bumping into someone, forgetting to do an errand. We can forgive ourselves for distracting thoughts and forgive the thoughts for distracting us. When our inner critic starts to speak, we forgive ourselves and forgive the critic for being so enthusiastic. We forgive ourselves for everything, from how we squeeze the toothpaste tube to how our voice quivered in that meeting.

Most of us have an inner critic that is so familiar we don't even recognize it. Continuous forgiveness helps bring that overlooked tension to the surface and allows it to relax in a welcoming embrace.

After a few days or a few months, those subtle tight places inside relax. Forgiveness starts to feel like simple kindness and compassion. We are ready to return to our regular practice.

Empirical Trials

As meditation practice deepens, what remains to be cleaned up is less generally applicable to everyone and more specific to our own particular temperament and proclivities.

It's natural to wonder about the nature of our experiences, have questions, and want guidance and confirmation. But sometimes there is no one around who can help us. The deeper our practice goes, the fewer the number of people who can give us useful guidance.

Gandhi subtitled his autobiography *The Story of My Experiments with Truth*. I like to think of meditation as experiments with the truth of awareness.

So if we have questions and no one to guide us, we can conduct empirical trials. Imagine what the guidance from a wise person might be. Then try it out — take your best shot at it. See what the results are. Try it another way. See what the results are. And so forth.

If we do this lightly, openly, patiently, and with a sense of humor, the chances are we'll find a good direction.

Asking "What Else?"

When our practice gets stuck or grows stale, it's often because our mind passed over something. As we Six-R the stuckness, the first *R*, Recognize, may need a little more time and attention to allow awareness to deepen. A simple way to do this is to ask, "What else is going on?"

For example, you might notice that the same conversation is repeating in a thought loop despite Six-R'ing it over and over. This usually means we're not seeing with enough breadth and depth.

So we ask, "What else is going on?" We're not trying to push thoughts or feelings aside. Rather, we let them be as they are and ask, "What else?"

This generous receptivity makes it easier to see multiple processes and qualities at once — explaining, worrying, figuring, fighting, anger, fear, hurt, worry, guilt, righteousness, and so on. — even if they contradict one another.

We don't anticipate or try to figure out what they might be. We just see what shows itself.

Then after pausing for a moment to allow the emergent thought, feeling, or quality to sink in, we gently Six-R. We don't Six-R to get rid of it but to make space for it and to allow its tension to dissipate naturally.

It's hard to fully notice tension without our grip on it starting to ease up. Or we can gently invite the tightness to soften. Trying to force relaxation can lead to more force than relaxation. So we soften into the tension to make sure we're not pushing it away.

With patience, eventually the inner space becomes peaceful. We let awareness rest in the peacefulness. At this point, our practice is no longer stuck or stale.

Sometimes a smile may arise spontaneously. When this happens to me, I often don't notice the smile for a few moments because it's so easygoing and I wasn't expecting it — it's not part of my self-image. It just arises on its own. If this happens to you, don't use it to push other, harsher qualities aside. Just let them all be there together.

The peacefulness of the smile may gradually absorb those harsher feelings into a tender aliveness that has fewer and fewer boundaries. This is a hint of enlightenment. Nothing is excluded. Everything is a part of everything.

As we rest in the immediate waves, we're also resting in a larger ocean. As the poet Babcock put it, we "rest in the immediate as if it were infinity, which it is." This is the beginning of nondual awareness.

Nondual Awareness

Nondual practice can be cultivated in other ways. For example, when the mind is relatively quiet, we may look at awareness and sense someone (us) seeing something: There is a seer and there is what's seen.

From that quiet, we relax deeply and allow the space between the seer and the seen to diminish. They start to move closer together. If we keep relaxing, the seer and the seen may become one and the same. At this point there is no separation. There is just awareness without a separate person who is aware. This is nondual awareness.

In the suttas it's described as non-self (anattā) — a negation. But in experience, it is more of a oneness. This is "one-dual" awareness.

Moving Toward the Present

Another, similar practice is bringing awareness as close to the present as possible. In reality, because of the massive number of neurons in the cerebral cortex that process perception, by the time we become aware of something, it is at least a fraction of a second into the past.

When the mind is relatively quiet, we notice how far into the past the content of the mind is. If I'm reminiscing about an event earlier in the day, the mind may be several hours in the past. If I'm delighted about how great my meditation is going today (or upset about how terrible it is), awareness is still focused at least a moment back.

To bring awareness closer to the present, we have to let go of thinking itself. Trying to push thoughts away just creates more tension and a longer time gap. Rather, we just let the mind relax into a simple, effortless flow of phenomena. As this happens, the sense of the seer and the seen may start to merge. This is nondual awareness, or oneness. In the present there is just a single flow of phenomena.

Jhāna practice is another way to describe moving toward the present. In the seventh jhāna, awareness relaxes so deeply that it doesn't coalesce into separate objects. There is just a flow of phenomena rather than a string of separate things. The seventh jhāna is called "the realm of nothingness." But a better translation might be "no-thing-ness" because there is just a flow rather than separate things. There is so much ease and contentment that the mind doesn't divide experience into conventional categories.

In the eighth jhāna, the mind doesn't even feel compelled to assemble perceptions and memories. This is called "neither perception nor non-perception." Perception doesn't stop cold. But neither does it continue on in its old way. The fluidity of the seventh jhāna becomes a radical relaxing that is not exactly the end of perception but not exactly a continuation of it either. Awareness is more attuned to the *elements* of perception than to putting them together into the familiar categories or concepts.

When awareness moves fully into the present, categories of past and future, self and other, fade. Eventually awareness itself fades. This later stage is called nirodha, or the cessation of perception, feeling, and consciousness.

Invoking Oneness

Even when we experience nondual awareness, this side of enlightenment we will slide out of it — sometimes a little, sometimes a lot. Nevertheless, nondual practices can still be helpful. They leave an embodied memory trace of what oneness feels like. Bringing the memory of that feeling forward can invoke the sense of being a part of everything.

It's said that no two snowflakes are alike; each is unique. However, when the temperature of snowflakes rises above freezing, they all melt into similar drops of water that are indistinguishable from one another. In one context, they are different; in another they are the same. In a similar manner, we can feel our individuality and our deep interconnection at the same time. We can be aware of our relative duality and our absolute nonduality all at once. This helps us relax into a sense of freedom.

It can also help us not to get stuck on a self! This is the core of the Buddha's teaching. We have a conventional dualistic self that navigates the world. But it is nothing more than a (sometimes) helpful illusion. As awareness relaxes and opens, the various selves fade into oneness.

> *Consider all phenomena to be dreams.*
> *Be grateful to everyone.*
> *Don't be swayed by outer circumstances.*
> *Don't brood over the faults of others.*
> *Explore the nature of unborn awareness.*
> *At all times simply rely on a joyful mind.*
> *Don't expect a standing ovation.*
>
> – Atīśa
> *Seven-Point Mind Training*

7

Fluidity of Life

The usefulness of meditation — or any spiritual practice — is not found in how wise, peaceful, or illuminated we feel sitting on a *zafu* with our eyes closed. It's in how clearly and heartfully we relate to the rest of our life. Even if we meditate for four hours a day, that leaves twenty hours when we are not engaged in spiritual discipline. Fluidity of practice is hollow if it doesn't support fluidity of living.

Ultimately, we may all be different manifestations of the oneness of everything. But in the relative world, there is a you and a me and everyone else with whom we interact in our daily lives.

How do you rest in the waves of the ordinary world of friends and family, work, and play?

To contemplate this question, let's reflect on the following topics: (a) the burdens we all carry, (b) the good hearts beneath those burdens, and (c) the compassion that arises naturally when we see our burdens and good heart at the same time.

Night Guard

But first, a confession: I wear a night guard. It's a piece of plastic that fits snuggly on my upper teeth. My dentist said I need it because the wear pattern on my molars suggests that I grind my teeth at night.

When she told me this, I thought, *I don't grind my teeth. I'm a meditation teacher. Teeth grinding would look bad on my résumé. She's mistaken. Or maybe it's just a temporary thing.*

I didn't say that out loud. I just replied, "Let me think about it."

She said kindly, "Of course. It's your choice. Let me know what you decide."

So I went home and thought about it — for over a year. During that time I realized that many — maybe most — of her patients have night guards. *She must make a lot of money on them,* I thought.

As appealing as that explanation was, it didn't match what I knew of her. In the fifteen years I've gone to her, I've never caught a hint of her putting her finances above the well-being of patients. If I had to choose between thinking she was greedy and thinking I grind my teeth at night, grinding was a safer bet. So I consented to a night guard.

This episode forced me to acknowledge a simple reality: My resting state is worry. This shouldn't have been a surprise to me because I came into this life worrying.

Yes, I do remember my birth:

During a deep psychotherapy session many years ago, I lay on the carpet of my therapist's office doing breathing techniques to bring up distant feelings, memories, and impressions.

During this session, a faint image formed in my mind of being in a dark, cramped, and clammy place. Two gray bars descended and gripped my head on either side. I began moving through a constricted tunnel.

Then I saw a man in a white lab coat. He was short with red curly hair, freckles, and dark-rimmed glasses. Though he smiled, his eyes were cold. He didn't care about me at all.

There were other people around, but they were ghostlike blurs. I couldn't feel their presence. I was all alone with these distant, emotionless beings.

I had a very strong feeling. It wasn't exactly a thought. But if I were to put it into words, it would be, *Mistake! This is a mistake! This is the wrong place. I don't belong here. I've come into the wrong body and the wrong life. As I came through the universe, I should have turned left at Jupiter rather than right. Now I'm stuck here. What am I going to do? Mistake!"*

Lying on the floor in my therapist's office I didn't take these images literally. They were metaphors arising out of the deep worry I carried.

Several weeks later I told my mother about the images. She was silent for a few moments. Then she said, "I never told you, but you were a forceps delivery... And the doctor looked just as you described him. My regular doctor was on vacation when I went into labor. So the red-haired doctor only came in to oversee the birth. We didn't see him before or afterward. And at the time, I thought he would have preferred to be playing golf.

"They gave me scopolamine. It was a medication used often back then with women in labor. It stops the formation of memories. If I couldn't remember being in pain a moment before, then I'd relax. The pain would not build on itself as much. The body could still do the birthing contractions with me suffering less because I couldn't remember it.

"Since I couldn't remember, I wouldn't have been present for you. I didn't know what was going on during that time."

I grew up in a schizoid family. Especially my father and older brother had a flat, relatively emotionless affect. The lack of emotional connection was confusing. I didn't understand it. I felt alone.

Gradually I slipped into a depression. It was like a clay mask I didn't even know I was wearing. In childhood pictures, I always have a forlorn look in my eyes. Those pictures break my heart.

The chronic depression was diagnosed in my late twenties. It took another ten years of therapy, bodywork, and meditation to finally break free of it. But the worry inside me was subtler. Compared with the depression, it wasn't much at all. So it remained.

As my mind-heart got quieter in meditation, I began to see a bit of worry, urgency, or fretfulness coloring every thought. The most obvious sign of this was my needing a night guard in my sleep.

We Carry a Lot

We all carry a lot. Some of it comes from our early years. There are ways each of us adapted in order to survive childhood. Some of us worry. Others feel longing, anger, "stiff upper lips," or other tendencies.

Some of what we carry comes out of family dynamics.

Some of it comes in response to the world around us. Does anyone feel angst about President Trump? How do you feel about political polarization? The coronavirus pandemic? The kind of world we're leaving for our children and grandchildren? The environment? Climate change? The growing wildfire seasons? Coastal flooding? What else?

We all carry a lot.

Some of it we can lay down from time to time. Some of it becomes layers of a clay mask we wear without realizing it.

What can we do about it?

The first thing we can do is to not leap into trying to fix it. This may seem counterintuitive. The German philosopher Martin Heidegger put it this way: "Imagine an awareness that sees to the heart of suffering with no urge to fix anything. Imagine this awareness is the opposite of indifference."

> *Imagine an awareness that is deeply engaged and yet so loving that it has no need to control, change, or fix anything. When you see this way, what do you notice in the depths of that experience?*

John Travis, one of my teachers, tells a story about this and what we see inside.

Venice of the East

Bangkok used to be called the "Venice of the East" because of all its rivers and waterways. In the middle of the twentieth century, it was growing rapidly. The economic boom built tall buildings and big roads. The old waterways were getting paved over with concrete streets.

During this time of expansion, an old, dilapidated temple was in the way of progress. The temple contained a large clay statue of the Buddha that was inlaid with colored glass. It would have been unseemly in a Buddhist country to take a wrecking ball to the shrine.

So on May 25, 1955, crews arrived outside the old temple, Wat Traimit. They brought large cranes, pulleys, ropes, and chains to move the statue to a suitable location and free up the temple to be destroyed.

They were able to tie up the Buddha statue and lift it off its pedestal. But as it moved, the ropes broke and the statue crashed to the ground. Miraculously, the statue did not shatter into little pieces. But it did crack and a few small chucks of clay fell away.

As crews assessed the damage, they noticed shiny yellow metal deep in the cracks. What had appeared to be solid clay turned out to be just a layer of stucco. When they removed it, there was a solid gold statue that sat ten feet tall, weighed over five and a half tons, and was worth over $250 million.

In the weeks that followed, they pieced together the history of the statue from ancient records. The gold Buddha was probably cast about seven hundred years earlier. About two hundred years ago, the Burmese army was preparing to invade Thailand. The Thai monks were afraid the army would carry off the statue as war booty. So they carefully covered it in clay stucco to disguise its real value. They used colored glass inlay and paint to make the statue seem genuine.

With the chaos of war and the subsequent decline in Thailand, the underlying nature of the statue was forgotten until that fateful day in 1955 when the heart of the statue was exposed.

Underneath, we are all golden buddhas — or golden Jesuses, Mother Theresas, or Ghandis. And we have all been covered with clay stucco. Some of it is crude. And some of it is finely carved and decorated. But it gives little hint of the golden luminosity beneath.

When we come to meditation, there is nothing we need to create, fix, heal, or transcend. Most of us carry burdens that are best laid down. But underneath those burdens is a heart of gold. There is luminosity below the stuff we carry.

Compassion

I think Heidegger got it right when he said we don't need to be fixed. And I would take this one step further:

When we see our burdens and our luminosity at the same time, the heart naturally opens. And when we see another's burdens and the light within them, compassion for them wells up spontaneously.

Try it and see what you notice. What might that look like? What follows is an example from my own experience.

I woke up early one morning and sat up to meditate. My mind wandered off into stories.

With my newfound appreciation for how easy it is for me to worry without knowing it, I quietly asked myself, *Is there worry?*

And there it was — the fretfulness was obvious when I looked. To see this clearly, I had to let go of the content of the worry. There can be endless volumes of content and they would take lifetimes to explore. So, remembering Heidegger's comment (p. 123), I let awareness see into the depths of the feeling of anxiety itself without trying to lift a finger to fix anything.

The worry seemed like a herd of buffaloes in the distance. I could feel the rumbling hooves but couldn't make out individual animals. I could feel the tension of worry without the story lines. This was the essence of what the Buddha called "wise effort" — it's the essence of the Six Rs: seeing process without content.

As the awareness got stronger and clearer, the rumbling slowly faded into the distance, leaving a quiet, luminous glow in its wake. In that luminosity, the subject of the worry seemed irrelevant and hard to remember.

> *When discomfort arises within, rather than put it down or rush ahead to something else, imagine it floating gently in the center of your chest. Let the content and stories drift into the background as you notice the feeling and tension themselves. Rest gently in them.*

Fluidity of Self in Daily Life

As we've seen, there is a wide range of states and qualities of awareness we humans can experience. Death and resuscitation are on the subtle end of this range. In enlightenment, the sense of self is light and irrelevant and the feeling of contentment is vast. In nibbāna, the sense of self is gone. On the coarse end of the scale is raging paranoia, where the sense of self is dense, the feeling of threat is high, the emotions are in turmoil, and suffering is great.

I can't speak from personal experience about these extremes. Like most people, my experiences are fluid across the broad middle range.

For many people, the most common experiences in the upper range occur when they are out in nature. When I'm hiking in the High Sierra, my sense of self feels irrelevant. In his lecture "Walking," Thoreau said, "In the wilderness is the preservation of the world." Nature is indifferent to who we think we are. At times like these, we may find we don't care that much either. We just feel part of it all.

Another common experience at the subtle end of the awareness spectrum comes from gazing into the eyes of our newborn child – all roles and posturing fade into the timelessness of that contact. Other moments in the upper range include sexual orgasm, a quiet evening on a beach, getting lost in poetry or music, and deep meditation or contemplation, to name a few.

I suspect we have more moments of selflessness than we realize because the sense of self fades into the distance where we don't see it. Meanwhile the joy or contentment are so strong that we aren't cognizant of a self. We don't even notice.

For the purposes of spiritual training, rather than be concerned about self or non-self, it's helpful to just notice how fluid the sense of self actually is. It not only changes in content but it also changes in strength.

> *Notice how the strength of a sense of self waxes and wanes throughout the day.*

From Higher Self to Connectedness to Selflessness

I am surprised and amused at how often people will look back on their lighter moments and describe them as their "higher self." Even descriptions of a death experience often use this language. But I don't think using this term is helpful or accurate. The word *self* implies others – a self separate from others.

I invite you to look at your own moments in the subtle range of well-being. Did you feel yourself more separate from others or more connected to them?

And is *connected* the best word? Did you feel more "connected" or just a part of everything?

And if you felt part of everything, did that sense of belonging feel like a new invention? Or did it feel like a broad, gentle awareness that had been waiting quietly even when you didn't notice it because other things were clamoring for your attention?

Awareness is fluid. It waxes and wanes, shifts in depth and sensitivity. Or perhaps awareness just is, but tension waxes and wanes, giving the feeling of fluidity.

It doesn't help to push for what we think is best. Resting in unborn awareness means letting things be as they are and letting the flower of awareness open in its own way.

Whatever you notice, let it be as it is and return to wholesomeness. If what you are most aware of are external things, notice the attitude in the mind toward those things. Whatever the attitude, can you notice the quality of awareness looking at the attitude? This is the path of resting in the waves: letting things be as they are and noticing the subtler qualities behind that awareness.

> *Notice the attitude of mind that is noticing this very moment.*

Summary

Awareness is a fierce, nuanced, kind, and unrelenting teacher. It is the center of the Buddha's path to awakening. In the previous few chapters we looked at it as a source of both steadiness and fluidity. Let me summarize a few of the insights.

The whole point of awareness is knowing what's going on around us. All creatures, whether a single-celled organism or a complex human being, have a better chance of surviving if they know what to avoid and what to engage. So the content of awareness is rudimentary and vital and draws our attention.

However, perception is imperfect. Different sense organs pick up different information. Our systems can ignore, enhance, confuse, or distort this raw sense data. *What* we know is clarified by knowing *how* we know it — the process of awareness as well as the contents. Is the mind explaining, arguing, worrying, delighting, defending, bragging, etc.? Processes can distort. Seeing the processes clearly helps minimize the effects of these distortions.

So in meditation, emphasis is placed less on *what* we know and more on *how* we know.

Once we can see the process, it's easier to see the subtle qualities of awareness itself. Is it clear, foggy, expansive, sluggish, jittery, loose, etc.? Knowing the qualities helps clarify awareness even more. There is always some tension in awareness. As we see this, we can relax and let awareness get even clearer.

As we notice the qualities and relax the tension, we may become aware of awareness itself. We may see how it arises, shifts, and fades. As we are more aware of awareness, any tension around it may actually relax when it is not needed.

The difference between an enlightened mind and an unenlightened stone is that the expansive mind can be instantly aware of content, process, qualities, and awareness itself when needed. It is highly responsive without being compelled.

Deepening perception moves from content to process to qualities to awareness of awareness to fading of awareness itself to nibbāna. The Buddha's map of the jhānas describes the upper end of this spectrum in detail. The point of spiritual practice is training the mind to be responsive without being constrained. It is both stable and fluid.

That is the nature of inner freedom. It doesn't get us anywhere new as much as show us where we've always been. Now we have the wisdom to see what once eluded us.

> *"I can contemplate the sea, but waves make me uneasy;*
> *Milarepa, tell me how to meditate on waves."*
> *"If the sea's as easy as you say,*
> *Waves are just the sea's play.*
> *Let your mind stay within the sea."*
>
> *"I can contemplate the sky, but clouds make me uneasy;*
> *Milarepa, tell me how to meditate on clouds."*
> *"If the sky's as easy as you say,*
> *Clouds are just the sky's play.*
> *Let your mind stay within the sky."*
>
> *"I can contemplate my mind, but thoughts make me uneasy;*
> *Milarepa, tell me how to meditate on thoughts."*
> *"If your mind's as easy as you say,*
> *Thoughts are just the mind's play.*
> *Let your mind stay within your mind."*

– Milarepa
Advice to Palderbum

8

Fluidity of Fluidity

We humans are complex creatures who exist fluidly in many dimensions at once. We live in physical, emotional, mental, social, cultural, political, and spiritual realms. We also live in the worlds of intentions, aspirations, stories, and much more. These realms interact and influence one another in ways that are lawful, complex, and nuanced. We cannot be reduced to any one realm or dimension.

Our physical nature may seem the most substantive. But if we were to be placed naked into interstellar space, in a matter of minutes we'd be reduced to a lifeless collection of frozen crystals. We are embedded in an ecosphere of air, water, minerals, and billions of other creatures. Without this vast interdependent ecology, we cease to exist as a living organism.

In other words, we are swirls within swirls embedded in larger swirls of interdependence. We have no independent self apart from the web of life. There is no solid rock we can stand upon and declare, "This is the real me."

For example, our bodies grow out of a unique set of twenty to twenty-five thousand genes. But how and when genes are activated can be influenced by food, rest, pathogens, stress, and a multitude of other internal and external factors. In addition to our physical bodies we are relational creatures affected by those around us. When someone enters the room, if we're quiet and attentive, we can notice how we shift inside.

Our responses to others are also influenced by our social, cultural, political, and economic circumstances. Our memories shift depending upon our mood, social setting, and so on. If we look within to find our true self, we find an endless labyrinth with no final endpoint.

Two Truths

The Buddha alluded to all this when he described two truths: the relative and the absolute.

The relative truth refers to how we think about life in everyday situations: We are distinct individuals; we are responsible for our actions; practices can help bring out our potentials; and so forth.

The absolute truth refers to the web of life as a whole. It is the deeper reality. We may have relative differences, but in absolute terms we are movements within this field of life.

These two truths should not be confused with Plato's two realms. In Western philosophy, Plato contrasts the realm of ideal forms with the ordinary world of degenerate shadows of those ideals. Ideal forms are superior to the ordinary.

The Buddha didn't say the absolute was better or more real than the relative. Both are real. They just have different frames of reference and behave differently. To be fully alive and awake is to live with both truths as the mind-heart moves fluidly between them.

Perhaps only a Buddha can remain fully conscious of both truths at the same time. However, we can learn to travel between them. As we become facile in moving back and forth, we are less likely to confuse one with the other.

The phenomena we refer to as mind and self are nothing more than a stream of phenomena that have no discernible beginning or end. No matter what our thoughts and feelings are about the origin of mind and self, there are experiences that precede it. And no matter where we end up, there is something else that follows. The awakened mind rests comfortably in the ever-shifting flux of experience.

When we see all this clearly enough, we are content to let things be as they are. With this, suffering abates. Then we continue on. There is no final destination called "my enlightened self."

> *If you have a hint of absolute truth, don't hold tightly to it. If you see relative truth, hold it lightly. Practice moving back and forth between them.*

All goes onward and outward, nothing collapses
And to die is different from
What anyone supposed, and luckier.

– from "Leaves of Grass," Walt Whitman

Emptiness

Another way to express the two truths is with the Pāli term *sunyata* (or *shunyata* in Sanskrit). It is usually translated as "emptiness." However, the root of the word comes from the verb *si,* meaning "to swell." Relative reality is sunyata, like a bubble. A bubble is real. We can see it. But inside, it is vacuous. There is nothing below the surface.

To say our lives are relatively real doesn't mean they are completely an illusion. Our lives are real. The self is real. But it's real only in the way a bubble is real. It has a surface with nothing substantive within.

If we don't see the emptiness and instead base our lives on imagined solidity, then when the true nature of things is revealed, we will suffer. However, if we see that the world and the self are empty, we can live with them just fine. It requires a mind that is clear, a heart that is kind, and an awareness that is fluid.

> *What if the surface of life is real and the interior is open space? Can you look fiercely, gently, and openly into the emptiness?*

Rose Apple Tree

With this understanding of the two truths and emptiness, let's go back to the experience of fundamental fluidity and how it is cultivated. The Buddha's life gives us a clue.

When Siddhartha became a buddha, he remembered a moment from his childhood. His family had left him under a rose apple tree while they joined the spring ritual of the first plowing of the fields. Sitting in the shade of the tree, he felt how life was swirls within swirls of interdependence with nothing fundamentally separate from anything else. He effortlessly went into a deep and pervading calm.

The vision was too far from the way the people around him understood the world. So it faded from his conscious memory, though it remained hidden inside. It was part of what encouraged him to embark on his spiritual quest as a young man. Years later, when he sat under the bodhi tree and woke up, it didn't feel like a new revelation or new quality of mind. It felt like something he already knew deep down but had forgotten.

I suspect there are many among us who have had rose apple tree moments — moments when we tasted interrelatedness and deep calm but don't consciously remember them. But it affects us. It may have been part of what drew us to meditation.

When meditators share with me glimpses of oneness, I often ask, "Does this insight feel like a new revelation? Or does it feel like remembering something you once knew but somehow forgot?"

Typically they pause for a moment to reflect. Then they say, "It does feel more like a forgotten memory. If you'd asked me about it yesterday, the insight would have seemed esoteric. But now it seems simple and obvious — no big deal."

The Buddhist texts do not describe enlightenment as a place we get to but as the unraveling of the notion of a self that is separate from everything else. Enlightenment is not a place at which we arrive; it's the recognition that there is no self to be enlightened. In the Udāna 8.1, the Buddha described it this way:

> *There is, bhikkhus, that base where there is no earth, no water, no fire, no air; no base consisting of the infinity of space, no base consisting of the infinity of consciousness, no base consisting of nothingness, no base consisting of neither-perception-nor-non-perception; neither this world nor another world nor both; neither sun nor moon. Here, bhikkhus, I say there is no coming, no going, no staying, no deceasing, no uprising. Not fixed, not movable, it has no support. Just this is the end of suffering.*[10]

At any given moment we may be moving in an enlightening or unenlightening direction. But there's no

---

[10] Translation by John D. Ireland (Kandy; Sri Lanka: Buddhist Publication Society, 1997).

destination. There's no awakened rock for us to perch upon, just swirls within swirls. Enlightenment is not a destination but the recognition that there ultimately is not self to be enlightened.

When we meditate, rather than seek new understandings, it may be more helpful to relax and rest in open awareness without an agenda. Don't try to guide awareness. Let it settle deeply into intuitive receptivity. Then see what emerges.

> *Don't search for insights. Let them find you. Ask, "What did I know but forgot?" Then leave the door open.*

Emptiness of Fluidity

Here's an example of emptiness and fluidity:

I woke up a little after 3:00 a.m. As I rolled over to drift back to sleep, my mind clamped down on a phrase from an email. A friend had referred to me as a "tightly wound guy." I didn't like the phrase. It wasn't complimentary. But I knew there was truth in it. The fact that I was lying in bed obsessing about it illustrated the point.

I Six-R fairly automatically. But I knew getting up to meditate would help the Six Rs be more effective. And besides, I was too awake to go back to sleep.

I sat up in a chair. Lila, our cat, curled up in my lap. I recited the Refuges, Precepts, and Aspirations. The aspirations reminded me of the general direction of the practice: "I seek to observe the mind-heart without preference. I seek clarity and acceptance. I seek to relax any tension in the self. I rest in oneness."

The mind opened, softened, and settled into stillness.

Then, like a dog chewing a bone, it chomped down on the phrase "tightly wound." I Six-R'ed again. And again.

After a few minutes, "obsessiveness" replaced "tightly wound" as the bone of choice. Then the dog spit out that bone and grabbed another. Then another. It was clear that the phrases didn't cause the mind to tighten. Rather, the mind tightened and then looked for an excuse to chew on.

I became more interested in the chewing than in the bone itself. The various phrases, images, and stories faded into the background as I watched the mind chomp and release, tighten and loosen, get noisy and quiet, contract and expand, stiffen up and let down. The periods of quiet lengthened until I could feel the slight thickening in the mind, release it, relax, smile at the humor of it all, and return to radiating well-being before any content arose.

Was my mind wound or loose? Was it tight or fluid? The obvious answer was yes. It was both.

The mind is in flux as it drifts from topic to topic, from one static state to another, from loosening up to tightening down. Being fluid and being fixated are not mutually exclusive. In short spans of time, continuity is easy to imagine. In longer spans of time, fluidity is obvious. It's just a matter of time.

Constancy, fluidity, and mystery coexist. All can be welcomed. Even fluidity comes and goes.

Yes, even fluidity is fluid.

> *Like a tiny drop of dew, or a bubble floating in a stream;*
> *Like a flash of lightning in a summer cloud,*
> *Or a flickering lamp, an illusion, a phantom, or a dream.*
> *So is all conditioned existence to be seen.*
>
> – the Buddha
> *Diamond Sutra 32*

Epilogue:

Beyond Heroics

The gray sky hinted at the coming dawn as I awoke early one morning. I could have used more sleep, but I was wide awake. So I sat up to meditate. Lila, our cat, mewed and purred as she hopped onto my lap and curled up. I closed my eyes, recited the Refuges, and began mentally composing this epilogue.

It was a few minutes before I realized I was explaining rather than meditating. I Six-R'ed and returned to sending well-being into the world. For forty-five minutes, my mind drifted back and forth between ruminating, Six-R'ing, and meditating. As I became more aware, the stories and thoughts slipped into the background and the processes of thinking and musing came into the foreground.

Suddenly the mind dropped into deep silence. One moment it had been chatting. The next it was empty. There had been too much energy in the mind. Noticing the processes allowed the chatting to burn off excess energy. The Six Rs also helped. When energy was released and relaxed, awareness dropped into stillness all by itself.

After a while, familiar images arose again in the mind. I didn't hold on to them or push them away. I just noticed the processes — thinking, imagining, explaining — and Six-R'ed. The pictures faded. Other images arose and faded.

It was not a great sitting by conventional standards. But as I got up to engage the day, I realized I was smiling quietly. My mind felt ordinary yet slightly luminous.

Habits

We all have mental habits that are so familiar that we overlook them even when they are right under our noses. These are ways that the mind dulls or yearns or turns away. Rather than see these habits clearly, we quietly assume, *That's no big deal — it's just the way I am,* and turn attention elsewhere. We identify with these habits and move on.

Bringing more awareness to habitual tendencies does not feel glorious or heroic. Yet we can't free ourselves from confusion and suffering when they ramble around unchaperoned.

One of my mental habits is explaining things, like I did in that early morning sitting.

> *What are some of your habits? When your mind assumes, "That's just who I am," what is actually going on? Can you bring more kindness and clarity to those mental patterns?*

I used to think that the most important parts of the Buddha's meditation were "oh, wow!" moments of deep insight or exalted states. They do provide inspiration and motivation. But for every inspiring or heroic moment, there are ten or twenty moments like that morning when my mind plodded along in its old, familiar habits. Bringing these patterns out of the background and into the foreground may be the most helpful thing we can do to free ourselves from unnecessary inner disturbances.

This way of practice is neither flashy nor heroic. Rather than try to fix ourselves or transcend mundane awareness, we let the patterns play out as we bring more mindfulness and heartfulness to them. As awareness penetrates them, we see them more clearly. As we see them more clearly, we identify with them less. As we identify less, they fade into the background and dissolve. How we treat the everyday mind is more important than how flashy the inspirations are. The deeper the awareness goes into our ordinary consciousness, the clearer and simpler it becomes, and the freer we become.

Beyond the Plateau

In the early years of my practice, diligently staying with the sensations of the breath was helpful because sensations are always in the present. Some of the mind's speculating, imagining, and rehashing subsided as awareness stayed more in the moment. When I became familiar with the jhānas, staying with the qualities in the mind helped it to quiet even more.

These practices were heroic in the sense of me trying to overcome the mind's errant tendencies to roam hither and yon. But they only took me so far. Eventually my meditation plateaued.

I thought one way to improve my practice was to sit longer: perhaps four hours. Ironically, this ambitious plan quickly showed me the limitations of heroics. It revealed how much I'd been subtly holding my attention on the breath or uplifted states. I could do it for a few hours. But four hours? Even the most genteel striving was too tiring over longer stretches. I couldn't pull it off.

My choice was either to sit for no more than an hour or two or to let the mind do what it was going to do and to relax more deeply. I decided to give the longer sittings another try even if it meant drifting more.

It still required some effort to remember to be aware and present. But I didn't try to hold attention on an object. I let it roam where it would and did my best to simply and heartfully notice what it did. I became more interested in how the awareness moved than in forcing it onto a predetermined object. This allowed me to sit longer without getting antsy.

I was surprised that, in time, the mind calmed itself. Or more precisely, it just slipped naturally into deeper and deeper stillness, like on that morning meditating with Lila. Simply paying attention to what the mind was doing — thinking, explaining, complaining, ruminating — created an environment in which it became calmer and clearer.

I realized that when the mind wandered, it wasn't because it was bad. It just had too much energy. Wandering awareness allowed that excitement to run out without stimulating more of it. Attending to the stories, ideas, plans, and concepts, just triggered more energy. But if I let all those stories drift into the background as I patiently watched the processes in the mind, it settled down and eventually dropped into a deep stillness.

Reminders

To be sure, this didn't always work. Sometimes the daydreams went on and on. Sometimes the mind dropped into stillness, sometimes it dropped into an epic tale. The shift from controlled to uncontrolled awareness is deceptively simple and deceptively difficult. Here are a few reminders of techniques that support this shift. You won't need all of these. So pick a few:

• Notice *how* your mind is behaving rather than *what* it is focused on. Notice the processes in the mind — thinking, explaining, ruminating, complaining, daydreaming, etc. Let them be in the foreground. Meanwhile let the content — the story lines, ideas, to-do lists, etc. — drift into the background. Don't push the content away. That just creates aversion and tension.

• Another way to think of this is to let awareness be in the present, here and now. Stories and plans are always in the past or future or someplace other than right here. Be here now, gently and clearly.

• Shift away from controlling awareness to simply observing it.

• If the qualities of your mind seem elusive or hard to recognize, notice the processes instead. Once the processes are clear, the qualities will be easier to see.

• If there are any thoughts or images floating through your mind, relax into them.

• If your mind feels sticky, slightly edgy, or thick, relax into these qualities.

• Balance your mind. If it tends to try too hard, balance it by allowing awareness to relax enough to seem a bit lazy. If it tends to relax into dullness, balance it by bringing in enough energy to seem a little edgy.

• If your mind doesn't feel slightly glowing, invite luminosity to reveal itself.

• Patience. You don't have to fix the mind or take care of it. It is enough to relate to it with kindness and clarity. Then it will take care of you.

• Enjoy.

Getting to Where We Are

To awaken to what's already here, we don't change ourselves into something new. We don't even vanquish old habits. We just let clearer and clearer awareness seep into them until they recede and evaporate. Freedom is not a matter of getting to somewhere else. It's a matter of getting to where we are. In "Little Gidding," T. S. Eliot put it this way:

We shall not cease from exploration
And the end of all exploring
Will be to arrive where we started
And know the place for the first time.

When we arrive where we are, we don't find our true self. We realize there never was a self apart from everything. This feels simple and ordinary. Less of an "oh, wow!" and more of an "Of course." If there is no self, there is nothing to suffer. That doesn't free the self. It dissolves it. There's nothing left: no past, no future, no "there" apart from here.

Dōgen wrote:

To study the way is to study the self.
To study the self is to lose the self.
To lose the self is to be enlightened by all things.
To be enlightened by all things is to remove the barrier between self and other.

Beyond Heroics

Heroic meditation techniques and flashy results are good for Hollywood movies. Watching the mundane habits of the mind with kind, clear awareness can be humbling. And it is freeing.

Rather than aspire to spiritual heroics, we can aspire to be like the little duck. "He can rest while the Atlantic heaves, because he rests in the Atlantic." If you have a hint of absolute truth, don't hold it tightly. If you see relative truth, hold it lightly. Practice moving back and forth between them. "He reposes in the immediate as if it were infinity — which it is.... He has made himself part of the boundless, by easing himself into it just where it touches him" right now in this simple, ordinary moment.

Appendices

Inquiries

These inquiry questions are found in the text boxes throughout the text on the pages indicated.

1 Fluidity of Self

Index

Note: **bold page numbers indicate primary entries**, *italic numbers indicate quotations.*

Printed in Great Britain
by Amazon